RISKY BUSINESS:
SHARING HEALTH DATA
WHILE PROTECTING PRIVACY

EDITED BY: KHALED EL EMAM

The development and publication of this book has been sponsored by the Electronic Health Information
Laboratory (EHIL) of the Children's Hospital of Eastern Ontario Research Institute and Privacy Analytics, Inc.

Printed in the United States of America.

ISBN: 978-1-4669-8050-1 (sc)
ISBN: 978-1-4669-8051-8 (hc)
ISBN: 978-1-4669-8049-5 (e)

Library of Congress Control Number: 2013903647

Trafford rev. 02/26/2013

 www.trafford.com

North America & international
toll-free: 1 888 232 4444 (USA & Canada)
phone: 250 383 6864 ♦ fax: 812 355 4082

CONTENTS

vi

INTRODUCTION

Over the last six years I have been involved in the release of more than one hundred de-identified data sets involving hundreds of millions of records. During that process, my team and I have worked with many public and commercial organizations ranging from health insurers to EMR vendors to academic organizations, including research hospitals and disease registries. Through this work we learned important lessons and identified a set of issues many organizations struggle with when disclosing health data for secondary purposes.

I will use two examples to illustrate some of these issues. The first common issue that comes up is whether an organization should follow the US HIPAA Safe Harbor de-identification standard. You may expect this question to be unique to US-based organizations, but we found many organizations in Canada are using the Safe Harbor standard as well. After collecting data and conducting analysis, we came to the conclusion that Safe Harbor was only defensible in a narrow set of circumstances. In turn, this was the advice we gave to the organizations that used our services. HIPAA has a second standard that allows organizations to perform a more meaningful risk assessment. This is the Statistical Method (also known as the Expert Determination Method). A number of articles about Safe Harbor and HIPAA standards are included in this book.

Another example of an issue organizations struggle with is the use of data-masking techniques. We encounter many organizations that have implemented classic data-masking techniques. After these implementation projects are complete, they are still not sure if they are compliant with the regulations. At that point they ask us for help. Through these engagements we have developed a set of recommendations about the use of classic masking techniques to defensibly protect data. A number of articles analyzing data masking and highlighting its strengths and weaknesses will be found in this book.

We created the *Risky Business* newsletter, which Privacy Analytics began publishing in 2011. The goal of the newsletter was to package practical advice and recommendations, coming from us and other experts in the field, in a format that was accessible to a large segment of the community. This helps promote good practices to organizations we work with and beyond. The *Risky Business* newsletter has been well-received and now has a significant and targeted readership: those interested in health data sharing.

Sometimes we get asked why we do not publish some of these articles in more academic journals. The main reasons are speed and focus. We can quickly publish articles in the *Risky Business* newsletter (usually within four to eight weeks). The turnaround time for academic journals is much longer, and we would not be able to get material out in a timely manner. Secondly, the *Risky Business* newsletter allows us to be succinct and practical. The articles do not start with a review of all relevant literature on the topic, for example. Most busy practitioners do not want to read a ten-page literature review before getting to the key point of an article they are interested in. Therefore, the *Risky Business* newsletter provides a format in which we can rapidly disseminate practical information on health data sharing to our clients and collaborators, as well as the broader community interested in health data.

Over the two years of *Risky Business*'s publication, we have accumulated quite an impressive set of articles with good practical advice and recommendations based on years of experience. Packaging these articles in a single book makes them more accessible to organizations. We are very grateful to all of the experts who have contributed their valuable time to write articles for the newsletter.

While *Risky Business* has published more articles than are included in this book, we selected articles that followed particular themes we felt caused confusion or where more guidance was needed. They are a function of the period we are in and the challenges organizations sharing health data are facing today. We hope that every eighteen to twenty-four months we will be able to publish a new compendium of *Risky Business* articles.

We would love to get feedback from our readers about what you found useful and relevant, what can be improved, and which new areas we should cover. Please get in touch with us. We are also always looking for authors who would like to contribute interesting articles.

If you would like to register to receive future issues of the Risky Business newsletter, please visit http://www.privacyanalytics.ca/riskybusiness.asp

Khaled El Emam
Founder and CEO of Privacy Analytics, Inc.
Canada Research Chair in Electronic Health Information, University of Ottawa
kelemam@privacyanalytics.ca
kelemam@ehealthinformation.ca

SECTION I

The Health Insurance Portability and Accountability Act (HIPAA)

PROTECTING THE BENEFITS OF DE-IDENTIFIED HEALTH-CARE INFORMATION

Kirk J. Nahra

Originally published in the Washington Legal Foundation's
Legal Backgrounder, vol. 27, no.9 (June 8, 2012).

A Pennsylvania Federal District Court's recent decision in *Steinberg v. CVS Caremark Corp.*, 2:11-cv-02428 (E.D. PA Feb. 16, 2012), recognizes both the benefits of the uses and disclosures of de-identified health-care information and the primacy of the HIPAA regulatory structure for defining the appropriate rules for this information. The court's decision therefore is an important step in the ongoing battle to reinforce the beneficial uses of this information, and the decision takes the courts out of disputes about this data that already are defined by the appropriate regulatory process.

Background

The privacy rule established pursuant to the Health Insurance Portability and Accountability Act (HIPAA) created a series of obligations for health-care providers and health insurers related to the uses and disclosure of individually identifiable health-care information. These rules created particular situations where patient consent was presumed (in the areas of treatment, payment, and health-care operations), as well as certain public policy areas where disclosure of patient information was permitted for other public goals (such as establishing rules for disclosure in connection with fraud investigations, litigation, certain public health activities, and otherwise).

The HIPAA rules also created a set of standards for establishing when health-care information was no longer "individually identifiable"—or would be considered "de-identified." Where information met the regulatory requirements for de-identification, health-care information was considered de-identified by law, and therefore was no longer subjected to the HIPAA restrictions on the uses and disclosure of individually identifiable information. Because the "individual" component of this information had been removed, this de-identified information could then be used and disclosed for a wide variety of purposes (including research and public health purposes, as well as commercial purposes), without creating meaningful privacy risks for any individuals. De-identified information is used widely for these purposes in the United States and across the world.

This HIPAA framework has existed since the HIPAA Privacy Rule went into effect in 2003. Pursuant to this framework, identifiable health-care information is subjected to HIPAA restrictions, and de-identified information can be used for additional purposes that otherwise could be impermissible, not subjected to restriction under HIPAA. (There are, of course, also good privacy reasons to use de-identified information even for otherwise permitted purposes, whether pursuant to the idea of "minimum necessary" or simply as a means of avoiding or reducing the risk of a privacy or security breach, but this is more of an issue of data "minimization" than anything else.)

The HIPAA Privacy Rule acknowledges and supports the benefits of these uses of de-identified information while at the same time recognizes that any material privacy interests have been eliminated through this de-identification process. The HIPAA rules make clear the information we are talking about is "Health information that does not identify an individual and with respect to which there is no reasonable basis to believe that the information can be used to identify an individual is not individually identifiable health information" (see 45 C.F.R. § 164.514(a)). The US Department of Health and Human Services (HHS), in developing these standards, therefore, specifically wanted to ensure "the Privacy Rule would not be a disincentive for covered entities to use or disclose de-identified information wherever possible" (67 Fed. Reg. 14776, 14799 (Mar. 27, 2002)).

Litigation Background

Steinberg v. CVS Caremark was filed on behalf of individual consumers and a union benefit fund. The allegations involve two potential classes, comprised of pharmacy patients and third-party payors. It alleges sales of prescription information to data mining companies and to pharmaceutical manufacturers directly. This complaint asserts that the data being sold was derived from both consumers and third-party payors, contrary to law and to the relevant privacy notices.

These activities allegedly occurred "despite Defendants' public pronouncements as to the sanctity of both consumers' privacy and the physician-patient relationship." In addition to various general "public relations" statements about privacy identified in the complaint, the complaint also focuses on specific statements from the CVS Caremark Notice of Privacy Practices. It asserts that this notice "contains exactly zero information detailing the twin multi-million-dollar sale programs."

The core of the complaint is that CVS, "in direct contradiction to representations made by Defendants," has profited from the sale and dissemination of "confidential prescription information" obtained from patients and third-party payors. This allegedly constitutes unfair and deceptive practices and unjust enrichment.

In Count 1 (an alleged violation of Unfair Trade Practices), the Defendants allegedly omitted material facts from its disclosures whenever it sold a prescription and intentionally failed to disclose to consumers that it would be engaged in the sale of prescription data. The Complaint asserts that Defendants have engaged in fraudulent or deceptive conduct which creates a likelihood of confusion or misunderstanding.

In Count 2 (for unjust enrichment on behalf of a third-party payor class), the assertion is that CVS's receipt of funds through sale of prescription information is unjust in the circumstances; therefore, CVS was "unjustly enriched" to the detriment of the third-party payor class. Similarly, in Count 3 (also an unjust enrichment count, but this time on behalf of a patient class), the plaintiffs allege, with no additional detail, the restated allegations for the unjust enrichment claim involving the third-party payor class.

The Steinberg Decision

The decision by Judge McLaughlin rejects the plaintiffs' theories in their entirety and dismisses the complaint, with prejudice, relying primarily on her conclusions that the defendants "have not disclosed legally protected information." In addition, as plaintiffs "clarified" at oral argument, the court concluded that defendants "neither sold information entitled to legal protection nor made any misrepresentations on which the plaintiffs justifiably relied regarding the way that consumer information would be handled. In addition, the information the defendants sold to third parties does not carry a compensable value to the plaintiffs or constitute an invasion of privacy." Accordingly, the court dismissed all claims. In addition, "because the plaintiffs have not articulated a viable alternative theory of liability, the court's dismissal will be with prejudice."

In small part, the court's decision was based on continuing confusion from the plaintiffs about the basis for their claims. At oral argument, the plaintiffs (despite allegations to the contrary in the complaint) "conceded that the information sold by the defendants to third parties was de-identified within the meaning of HIPAA" (this concession was inconsistent with various assertions in the complaint).

Moreover, the court's decision reinforces the conclusion that the relevant HIPAA rules provide the appropriate yardstick for measuring the appropriateness of the plaintiffs' claims. For the unfair trade practices claim, the court concluded that both "disclosures" made by the defendants (certain communications about the patients made to their treating physicians and certain disclosures of de-identified information to third parties) were "permissible disclosures" under the HIPAA rules. Because these disclosures were permitted by the applicable rules, and the relevant privacy notices made clear that the defendants could make disclosures that were permitted by law, the court found no basis for plaintiffs to assert an unfair or deceptive trade practices claim.

Just as important, however, the court also rejected the plaintiff's standing under this count, as the plaintiffs demonstrated no justifiable reliance on any statements by the defendants and suffered no financial loss. The court found that "plaintiff's claim that he suffered a loss as a result of the sale of his information is without factual support in the complaint." The complaint "contains no allegations that [plaintiff] would have sought to fill his prescriptions elsewhere had he known of the defendants' practices.

Nor does [plaintiff] allege that the defendants' actions deprived him of the opportunity to sell his information to data aggregation firms directly." Therefore, the plaintiff "has not shown that he was harmed by the defendants' actions," and therefore lacked standing to pursue this claim.

The court also rejected the idea that any financial benefit to the defendants was somehow unjust in these circumstances, as the plaintiffs "have not shown that the information disclosures by the defendants caused them to suffer an ascertainable loss. For related reasons, they cannot show that they conferred a benefit on the defendants or that retention of any benefit would be unjust under the circumstances."

The court added:

The relationship between the plaintiffs and defendants was one wherein the plaintiffs provided certain information in exchange for the provision of pharmacy services. Under the circumstances, the plaintiffs could have no reasonable expectation of being compensated for the information related to that transaction because that information carries with it no compensable value at the individual level. The plaintiff paid the defendants to fill prescriptions, and the defendants did so. Retention of any benefit accruing to the defendants from the de-identification, aggregation, or sale of patient information could not be considered unjust under the circumstances.

Implications

Questions about the use and disclosure of de-identified information continue to be raised, both in litigation and through the regulatory process. The Steinberg decision addresses several of these key issues and (presumably) creates significant precedent to shut down future claims involving this information. Specifically, the court's decision makes clear that

- disclosure of information that has been de-identified pursuant to HIPAA is permitted by law; because this information has been "de-identified," the individuals whose information was the original source of this de-identified data have no material privacy or monetary interest remaining in the data; and
- the courts should not intervene to address challenges to de-identification practices beyond the HIPAA standards, including the evaluation of whether information properly has been de-identified (as that is an issue for the regulatory and HIPAA enforcement process).

These findings should serve both to stem the tide of future litigation in this area and to protect the many benefits of the use and disclosure of de-identified health-care information, for public health and research purposes, as well as various commercial purposes. These findings—which are clearly consistent with the approach taken in the HIPAA Privacy Rule—conclude there is no material privacy interest when otherwise personal information has been de-identified. This approach represents a reasonable and appropriate balance between the Privacy Rule itself—which protects individual privacy interests—and the demonstrable benefits of the use and disclosure of de-identified data, both for clear "public benefit purposes" such as research and public health and for other commercial purposes.

PROBING BENEATH DATA BREACH HEADLINES: THE RIPPLE EFFECTS OF HEALTH DATA STEWARDSHIP

Dennis Melamed

It may feel like health care is under regulatory attack for the way it manages patient data, and in many ways it is true. Few industries come under such intense government supervision over every mundane operational detail.

However, American health-care organizations that focus only on the Health Insurance Portability and Accountability Act (HIPAA) and the Health Information Technology for Economic and Clinical Health (HITECH) Act compliance fail to understand the more profound and pervasive operational consequences the attention to data stewardship has spawned.

Not-So-New Initiatives

It has been fifteen years since HIPAA became law, and it has been almost eight years since the US Department of Health and

Human Services' (HHS) Office for Civil Rights (OCR) started enforcing the law's privacy and security provisions.

In that time, health care has taken substantial steps to gain control over patient data. The industry has taken its responsibilities seriously, and the substantial number of cottage industries that have developed around security and confidentiality are a testament to that fact. At the same time, it appears health care continues to address these issues as ones of compliance and not ones of operational necessity.

We Didn't Get It Right the First Time

The industry's attitude shifted with the passage of the HITECH Act. The immediate effect was to create a breach notification program that would publicly embarrass health care for its failure to control patient data and to make the industry pay something for its mistakes.

However, It Still Seems We Have a Long Way to Go

An analysis by health information privacy/security alert of the breaches affecting more than 500 patients through November 17, 2011, is revealing. There have been 364 breaches affecting almost 18 million patients. The primary causes have been extremely low tech: theft and loss. More than half of these breaches were attributed, at least in part, to the theft of records or equipment containing records. At least another 50 were attributed in part to the loss of records. Another 18 breaches were caused by improper disposal. What is even more telling is that paper records were involved in 86 breaches.

What's Not Making Headlines

The breach notification program only reports incidents that affect more than five hundred patients. That is far from the end of the story. The HITECH Act requires health-care organizations to self-report incidents affecting fewer than five hundred patients. These have been easy to overlook, but that is a terrible mistake.

OCR has received tens of thousands of these reports since February 2010. The agency observed that many of these reports deal with day-to-day glitches can be expected in a multitrillion-dollar industry. But some of these incidents have been significant.

An OCR regional office zoomed in on two incidents that affected more than one hundred patients. One involved the loss of a backpack that contained a written diary of a medical resident, who tracked patients and procedures for review by the resident's advisors. The other breach involved the theft of one operating-room laptop that contained records on more than one hundred patients. In response to the reported breaches, OCR conducted an intensive review of many of the organization's policies on computer security and physical security and insisted on changes in operations.

Self-Reported Breaches versus Patient Complaints

To put the smaller breaches into perspective, it is important to understand the complicated nature of OCR's medical privacy enforcement. Before the breach notification requirements, HIPAA required OCR to establish a system in which patients could lodge complaints about possible HIPAA privacy violations. As of October 31, 2011, OCR has received 65,401 complaints since this program began in April 2004. Of those, 22,075 fell within OCR's HIPAA jurisdiction. That meant OCR had to investigate the complaint. Of those complaints, 14,768 required health-care organizations to change policies.

In the HITECH Act context, OCR said in recent budget documents that if the self-reported breaches were submitted as patient complaints, the agency would have to investigate more than twice the number of incidents it does now. The agency acknowledges that the limiting factor in pursing all self-reported small breaches is the lack of enforcement resources for the OCR regional offices.

A good example of a privacy complaint that also would have been a self-reported breach would be the one-million-dollar resolution agreement with Massachusetts General Hospital in February 2011. The incident involved an employee who lost paper records on 192 patients, including patients with HIV/AIDS.

The Pervasive Effects of HIPAA and HITECH

Because health data stewardship is at the heart of the billions upon billions of everyday activities that occur within health care, the effects on the workforce tend to get downplayed. To be sure, compliance requires workforce training, and most people understand that.

However, the notification provision for smaller breaches also means small errors can become federal cases—by definition. Many of these errors are no longer something that can be fixed by an informal conversation with an employee. When a smaller breach is reported, OCR wants to see how the organization fixed the problem. That typically means more training or some kind of employee sanction. Sometimes that means firing the employee. This has not been without its challenges as well.

In recent years, health-care employees have increasingly lodged a host of legal challenges over employers' methods for disciplining employees for HIPAA violations. That may mean the days of suspending doctors while firing nurses for snooping into celebrity files may be over.

The overarching point, however, is that it is in this human resources sphere that health-care management should finally realize the health data stewardship requirements are more than about HIPAA or the HITECH Act. They are about an operational environment that takes the protection and use of its most important resource—patient data—as seriously as an operations issue.

Relevant Reading

1. Department of Health and Human Services, http://www.hhs.gov/ocr/privacy/hipaa/administrative/breachnotificationrule/breachtool.html, 2011
2. Department of Health and Human Services, http://www.hhs.gov/ocr/office/index.html, 2011.

HIPAA SECURITY SPOT AUDITS BEGIN: "CHICKEN LITTLE" AND ANNUAL TRADITIONS

Kenneth Rashbaum, Esq.

The Health Information Technology "Chicken Littles" who have been writing and saying for the past year that the Office for Civil Rights (OCR) of the US Department of Health and Human Services (HHS) will ramp up Health Insurance Portability and Accountability Act (HIPAA) security enforcement have been proven at least partially correct. Like the annual holidays, the audits were inevitable and sure to become a frequent tradition.

On December 1, 2011, OCR published its sample audit letter, indicating that the receiving entity will be the subject of an audit, conducted by KPMG LLP, within thirty to ninety days of receipt of the letter. Approximately 20 of these letters went out, mostly to health-care providers but some to health plans and health-care clearinghouses. OCR intended to audit 150 entities in this first "pilot" audit project.

News of the audits was sprung in a press release from OCR on November 8, 2011, compounding the flurry of preparations and activities at a time when many are focused on the coming holidays. The audit program, authorized by the Health Information Technology for Economic and Clinical Health (HITECH) Act, is as wide as it is deep, reaching HIPAA business associates such as law firms and HIT consultants as well as traditional covered entities such as health plans and providers. It is anticipated that the auditors will, before arriving on site, request documentation in the form of policies and procedures as to technical, administrative and physical safeguards for Protected Health Information (PHI). They may also interview executive personnel and randomly selected "front-line users" such as physicians, nurses, and billing staff. A comprehensive review of security and operations protocols should also be expected.

The HIT "Chicken Littles" need not be proven 100 percent prescient, though, because now that covered entities and business associates have been forewarned, they can take steps to prevent the sky from falling. First, they should conduct and document (or update) their HIPAA Security Risk Analysis. A current documented risk analysis is required by the HIPAA Security Rule 45 C.F.R. § 164.308(1) (ii) (A) and will be undoubtedly one of the first items requested by the auditors. The time to begin the analysis is not when the entity has received the audit letter. A comprehensive HIPAA Security Risk Analysis is an interdisciplinary initiative comprising IT, health information management, risk management, and legal and clinical departments (front-line HIT users). It is often facilitated by experienced outside counsel who will also sign the analysis documentation.

The timing of the spot audit project may have been accelerated by the recent spate of health information security breaches in the United States. Contrary to what one might expect—that these incidents occurred at smaller institutions that perhaps did not have robust HIPAA protocols—these breaches took place at such well-known academic medical centers as Stanford University Hospital, UCLA Health System (twice), Johns Hopkins Hospital,

Massachusetts General Hospital, and Brigham and Women's Hospital. Penalties levied by the Office of Civil Rights have been in the hundreds of thousands of dollars.

In the audits, OCR was going to seek evidence the institution has taken reasonable steps to prevent data breaches to fashion a protocol for response to and remediation of breaches. The auditors were going to, of course, review the information systems, but they were also going to look for evidence that security is an integral part of the business. The time to document such efforts, in the HIPAA Security Risk Analysis and pertinent protocols, is before an audit letter is received.

Relevant Reading

1. Department of Health and Human Services, OCR press release, http://www. hhs.gov/ocr/privacy/hipaa/enforcement/audit/index.html.
2. Department of Health and Human Services, OCR Sample Audit Letter, http://www.hhs.gov/ocr/privacy/hipaa/enforcement/audit/sample-ocr_notification_ltr.pdf.
3. Department of Health and Human Services, OCR, HIPAA Security Rule, 45 C.F.R. § 164.308(1)(ii)(A), http://www.hhs.gov/ocr/privacy/hipaa/understanding/srsummary.html.
4. Department of Health and Human Services, OCR, Fiscal Year 2012, *"Justifications of Estimates for Appropriations Committees"*, http://www.hhs.gov/about/FY2012budget/ocr_cj_fy2012.pdf.

ATTESTATION: STRENGTHENING SATISFACTORY ASSURANCES OF THE HIPAA BUSINESS-ASSOCIATE AGREEMENT

Grant Peterson, JD

Today, health-care organizations are faced with a growing trend of sharing confidential health information with vendors (business associates) in order to meet critical business needs. However, from a risk management perspective, little if any assessment of business-associate compliance is performed; leaving little assurance of sound compliance practices by the business associate handling patients' confidential health information.

New Regulations for Business Associates

Much of the concern results from sweeping changes in 2009 to the privacy and security regulations of the Health Insurance Portability and Accountability Act (HIPAA) of 1996, resulting from the Health Information Technology for Economic and Clinical

Health (HITECH) Act. The HITECH Act imposes additional privacy and security rules on business associates. For example, the HITECH Act applies the administrative, physical, and technical safeguard requirements of the security rule to business associates, including obligations related to policies, procedures, implementation, and documentation.

In addition, new data breach notification requirements within the HITECH Act now apply to covered entities and business associates, requiring patient notification of any unauthorized acquisition, access, use, or disclosure of their unsecured protected health information. Moreover, increased civil and criminal penalties now apply to both parties for violations of HIPAA privacy and security requirements and authorize state attorneys general to bring civil actions on behalf of state residents adversely affected or threatened by such violations.

Studies Underscore Enhanced Due Diligence

As evidence of the potential concern for liability that may be unfolding, HIMSS (Healthcare Information and Management Systems Society) Analytics produced a 2009 report: "Evaluating HITECH's Impact on Healthcare Privacy and Security." The study reported that "business associates, those who handle private patient information for healthcare organizations—including everyone from billing, credit bureaus, benefits management, legal services, claims processing, insurance brokers, data processing firms, pharmacy chains, accounting firms, temporary office personnel, and offshore transcription vendors—are largely unprepared to meet the new data breach related obligations brought on by the HITECH Act. Business associates lag behind in all areas that were tested in this survey to measure awareness of the privacy requirements of the HITECH Act. Over 30 percent of business associates surveyed did not know the HIPAA privacy and security requirements have been extended to cover their organizations' data breach related obligations included in the HITECH Act."

Now, a recent patient privacy and data security study underscores the significance of the problem. In December 2011, the Ponemon Institute, a privacy and information management research firm, released its finding, *Second Annual Benchmark Study on Patient Privacy and Data Security*, reporting, "Despite increased compliance with the HITECH Act and other federal regulations, healthcare data breaches are on the rise . . . eroding patient privacy and contributing to medical identity theft. On average, it is estimated that data breaches cost benchmarked organizations $2,243,700."

In addition, a key finding from the study indicates that "96 percent of all healthcare providers say they have had at least one data breach in the last two years. Most of these were due to employee mistakes and sloppiness—49 percent of respondents in this study cite lost or stolen computing devices and 41 percent note unintentional employee action. *Another disturbing cause is third-party error, including business associates, according to 46 percent of participants*" (emphasis added).

Business-Associate Agreement

HIPAA requires that, "A covered entity [healthcare organization], in accordance with §164.306, may permit a business associate to create, receive, maintain, or transmit electronic protected health information on the covered entity's behalf only if the covered entity obtains *satisfactory assurances*, in accordance with §164.314(a) that the business associate will appropriately safeguard the information" (emphasis added).

The answer to "satisfactory assurances" has been the use of a business-associate agreement between the covered entity and the business associate, obligating the business associate to protect confidential health information. However, with the recent

HITECH Act requiring business associates to meet new obligations including the HIPAA Security Standards, Data Breach Notification requirements and increased penalties, covered entities feel the need to increase their due diligence of the business associate.

While HIPAA does not require the covered entity to "monitor" or validate the business associate, nevertheless, healthcare organizations are concerned that business associates are compliant with the new HITECH Act requirements and have begun exploring new ways to strengthen the satisfactory assurances of business associate compliance.

Attestation: A Validation Tool

Attestation has served as a valuable tool to validate a process or event in a broad range of services, including legal, financial and healthcare. As a tool, attestation is flexible in design and may be customized around a set of requirements and offered as formal process using assessors or developed for self-assessment.

Attestation is currently used in the Centers for Medicare and Medicaid Services (CMS) Electronic Health Record (EHR) Incentive Programs to provide a financial incentive for the "meaningful use" of certified EHR technology to achieve health and efficiency goals. In the case of Medicare eligible professionals and hospitals, these organizations will have to demonstrate meaningful use through CMS' web-based Registration and Attestation System. The Registration and Attestation System, sets meaningful use objectives for healthcare organizations to legally attest that they have successfully demonstrated meaningful use and therefore eligible for the incentive program.

Another example of attestation application is used within the Payment Card Industry (PCI). PCI has developed a security standard that includes requirements for security management, policies, procedures, network architecture, software design and other critical protective measures. This comprehensive standard is intended to help merchants proactively protect customer account data. PCI Security Standards Council offers comprehensive standards and a framework of specifications to help merchants ensure the safe handling of cardholder information. To assist merchants validate their compliance, the PCI Security Standards Council has created a self-assessment questionnaire for certain levels of merchants. The self-assessment certifies the merchants level of eligibility, validates compliance status and an action plan for non-compliant status. Annual self-assessments are required of the merchants.

The examples above represent proven use of attestation in a variety of formats applied to large populations. Like CMS and PCI applications, HIPAA and HITECH Act standards also provide a framework of existing specifications that healthcare organizations may use to develop an attestation of compliance for self-assessment questionnaire. In other cases of business associates handling large volumes of protected health information, the healthcare organization may create an on-site audit requirement using an independent assessor. The healthcare organization would update their business associate agreements to adopt new attestation requirements.

For healthcare organizations faced with the growing trend of sharing protected health information with business associates and the desire to strengthen "satisfactory assurances" of compliance, the attestation model may be the key to proactive risk management.

Relevant Reading

1. HIMSS Analytics and ID Experts, *"Evaluating HITECH's Impact on Healthcare Privacy and Security,"* http://www.himssanalytics.org/docs/ID_Experts_111509. pdf, HIMSS Analytics, 2009.

2. Ponemon Institute, *"Second Annual Benchmark Study on Patient Privacy & Data Security,"* http://thielst.typepad.com/files/2011-ponemon-id-experts-study.pdf, December 2011.

3. Health Information Privacy/Security Alert's HIPAA & Breach Enforcement Statistics Analysis of OCR Data, http://www.melamedia.com/HIPAA.Stats.home.html, December 17, 2011 - January 17, 2012.

4. Department of Health and Human Services, *"Summary of the HIPAA Security Rule"* http://www.hhs.gov/ocr/privacy/hipaa/understanding/srsummary.html, Accessed January 2012.

5. Centers for Medicare and Medicaid Services, *"Attestation, Centers for Medicare and Medicaid,"* https://www.cms.gov/EHRIncentivePrograms/32_Attestation.asp, Accessed January 2012.

SECTION II

Data Breaches

YOUR MOTHER WAS RIGHT: YOU WILL BE JUDGED BY THE COMPANY YOU KEEP

Rebecca Herold

The idiom "You will be judged by the company you keep" is still appropriate today, especially when talking about privacy breaches and considering who the public, and often the law, sees as ultimately responsible for lack of safeguards that led to the breaches. Consider the Saint Barnabas Health Care System in New Jersey. They've had not one but two significant privacy breaches within the span of a year. Of note is that each was a breach that occurred within business partners.

We can learn from their pain by looking at these breaches. First, here is an overview of each incident:

- May 10, 2010: While doing an audit of the Saint Barnabas Health Care System, a KPMG auditor lost an unencrypted flash drive that contained the health-care and personal information of around 4,500 patients. There were reportedly encryption policies in place, but in this case those policies had not been followed.

- June 24, 2011: A MedAssets employee left an unencrypted hard drive containing the health information of 82,000 patients of six hospital systems they were auditing in a parked car outside a restaurant. The drive contained 6,200 patient records of Saint Barnabas hospital alone. While the employee dined, a crook stole the hard drive.

In the United States, under the HIPAA Act, KPMG and MedAssets are considered business associates of the hospital system, so the hospital system had to break the bad news to those affected in each of these incidents. It is possible many of their patients were provided notices just one year apart about a breach involving their health information result. Even if HIPAA did not apply, it is best for the primary organization that originally collected the personal information to inform the individuals whose personal information was breached since they have the direct relationship with those individuals.

These examples should really highlight not only the need to ensure that your organization has effective safeguards and privacy breach prevention and response measures in place but to ensure all your business partners have them in place as well—not only health-care organizations, but every organization that collects, processes, or stores personal information. Are your business partners effectively protecting the information you've entrusted to them? Will they respond appropriately in the event a privacy breach does occur?

Here are some proactive steps you can take to ensure your business partners are protecting the information you've provided:

1. **Define personal information.** Make sure your business partners' definition falls within your organization's definition.
2. **Know how personal information is used.** They need to know who collects, processes, stores, or accesses personal

information, in addition to documenting how it is used. They should also have a position formally documented as being responsible for these activities.

3. **Know where personal information is kept.** They should have storage locations, including mobile endpoints and employee-owned storage locations, identified. These should include third parties to whom they have entrusted the storage of information. Ask them to establish an inventory of personal information and to keep it up-to-date.

4. **Know data-retention requirements.** They should have documented data-retention requirements as specified by the organizations they do business for, as well as within their applicable regulations, such as HIPAA in the United States and by PHIPA in Ontario. It would be beneficial to have these retention requirements incorporated into the personal information inventory.

5. **Limit access to PHI.** They should have safeguards implemented to restrict access to only those who have a business need to access the information for business purposes. Access should not be given beyond the purposes for which the information was collected.

6. **Implement appropriate safeguards.** Every business partner should conduct regular risk assessments and then implement effective safeguards to appropriately mitigate the identified risks in accordance with documented policies and procedures.

7. **Document breach response plans.** Every business partner needs to have a documented plan in place detailing the steps to identify and respond to a breach. This includes documenting how and when they will notify your organization if the breach involves your information. Simply saying, "We'll call Chris" does not qualify as an acceptable breach response plan. I actually had a business associate

tell me this during one of my audits of their information security and privacy program!

8. **Communicate.** Every business partner should communicate about information security and privacy policies, procedures, and how to conduct the associated activities previously described, through regular training and ongoing awareness communications. These actions need to be supported with the appropriate technology tools and appropriate control processes.

Encryption is an example of an effective type of safeguard the Saint Barnabas Health Care System should have required of their business partners and then verified. If their business partners could not encrypt the data, the Saint Barnabas Health Care System should have de-identified the data before providing the information to the business partners, if this would have been a feasible option.

ANATOMY OF A DATA BREACH, PART 1: DATA PRIVACY REGULATIONS, PENALTIES, AND STATISTICS

James J. Giszczak and Dominic A. Paluzzi

In today's electronic age, with personal and financial information and protected health information stored on computers, laptops, the Internet, and other miniature media devices, and with the rise of identity theft, individuals are more concerned than ever about protecting their personal information and protected health information. Increasingly, companies have become targets, internally and externally, for people misappropriating this information for improper purposes.

"Anatomy of a Data Breach" is a three-part series of articles that will discuss data privacy and the rapidly changing laws that entities must adhere to and the challenges they face through the compliance process. This first article will address the general concepts of data security, stunning statistics, critical privacy laws and penalties for noncompliance. The second article will feature proactive measures and requirements to minimize the risk of a data breach in your organization. Finally, the third article will address the immediate and appropriate actions to take once a breach occurs.

What is most important in the data privacy arena is for your organization to partner with vendors that have significant experience advising clients on best practices, security, and storage policies; dealing with data breaches; and complying with state and international data security laws. It's important to find a balance between the information requirements of your organization and the individual rights of your employees, customers, and third parties. This area of law is rapidly changing, and it's critical that the complex privacy laws are both understood and followed.

Questions to Consider:

- Does your company have a written information security program?
- Have you established clear data security procedures?
- Does your company have an incident response plan?
- Are you aware of the myriad of state, federal, and international laws that require data breach notification?
- Do you have appropriate IT and electronic policies concerning personal or other sensitive information, whether in hard copy or stored on laptops or other portable devices?
- Does your company properly protect its personal information with confidentiality agreements for its employees, vendors, and visitors?
- Does your company properly train its employees on its data security program and policies?

If you just read these questions and are asking yourself, "What is an incident response plan?" or "What is a written information security program?" you are not alone. Let's discuss why we even need to be talking about data privacy in the first place.

What Data Is Protected and Who Is Impacted?

By state and federal statute, personal information (PI) or personally identifiable information (PII) refers to unique identifiers such as an individual's social security number, driver's license number, credit card numbers, credit report history, passport number, tax information, and banking records. Protected Health Information (PHI) refers to medical records, health status, provision of health care, and payment for health care.

Every industry is at risk when it comes to data privacy, but some are more critical, such as billing companies, education, insurance, staffing, health care, retail, manufacturing, accounting, financial services, legal, pharmaceuticals, and government/military. These industries are most at risk due to the amount of sensitive PI and PHI they either own, license, or otherwise have access to and/ or control.

Startling Statistics

The breach of more than 544,664,595 records have been reported since 2005[1] A Ponemon Study has recently found the average cost of a data breach is $214 per compromised record, which is broken down as follows:

Activity	Percent of Total Cost	Dollar
Investigation and Forensics	11 percent	$23
Audit and Consulting Services	10 percent	$21
Outbound Contact	5 percent	$10
Inbound Contact	6 percent	$13
Public Relations/Communications	1 percent	$2
Legal Services—Defense	14 percent	$30
Legal Services—Compliance	2 percent	$4
Free or Discounted Services	1 percent	$2
Identity Protection Services	2 percent	$4
Lost Customer Business	39 percent	$83
Customer Acquisition Cost	9 percent	$19
Total	100 percent	$214

Source: http://www.ponemon.org/index.php

Of the attacks, 85 percent are not even considered difficult, and 96 percent are avoidable through simple or intermediate controls[2].

So what is the incentive for a criminal to have access to your PI through either a low-tech breach or via hacking into a computer network? The value of your stolen data on the black market is quite surprising:

Overall Rank		Item	Percentage Sold on Black Market		2010 Price Ranges for Stolen Data
2010	2009		2010	2009	
1	1	Credit Card Information	22 percent	19 percent	$0.07-$100
2	2	Bank Account Credentials	16 percent	19 percent	$10-$900
3	3	E-mail Accounts	10 percent	7 percent	$1-$18
4	13	Attack Tools	7 percent	2 percent	$5-$650
5	4	E-mail Addresses	5 percent	7 percent	$1/MB-$20/ MB
6	7	Credit Card Dumps	5 percent	5 percent	$0.50-$120
7	6	Full Identities	5 percent	5 percent	$0.50-$20
8	14	Scam Hosting	4 percent	2 percent	$10-$150
9	5	Shell Scripts	4 percent	6 percent	$2-$7
10	9	Cash-Out Services	3 percent	4 percent	$200-$500 or 50 percent-70 percent of total value

Source: http://www.symantec.com/threatreport/

Critical Privacy Laws and Standards

As a result of the increased frequency of data thefts and breaches of PI and PHI, the data privacy regulations are voluminous and onerous. There are at least thirty-five federal laws with data protection or privacy protections. Forty-six states, the District of Columbia, Puerto Rico, the Virgin Islands, and numerous foreign countries have enacted legislation requiring notification of security breaches involving PI and/or PHI. Relative to the forty-six state statutes, it is the residence of the affected individual that determines the applicable notice law, regardless of whether the entity has a business physically located in that state.

A highlight of some of the critical privacy laws and standards currently in effect are as follows:

- **Health Insurance Portability and Accountability (HIPAA) Act of 1996**
    - requires health-care providers to ensure the confidentiality of all protected health information (PHI)
- **Health Information Technology for Economic and Clinical Health (HITECH) Act**
    - imposes new notification requirements on covered entities, business associates, and vendors if a breach of unsecured PHI occurs
- **Gramm-Leach-Bliley Act (GLBA)**
    - requires financial institutions to safeguard security of customer information/records and protect against unauthorized access of same
- **Federal Trade Commission Red Flags Rule**
    - requires financial institutions and creditors to implement written identity theft programs to identify theft, prevent crime, and anticipate damages
- **Identity Theft Enforcement and Restitution Act (ITERA)**
    - victims of identity theft allowed to recover an amount equal to value of time spent by victim to remediate the intended or actual harm incurred
- **Payment Card Industry Data Security Standards (PCI DSS)**
    - requires organizations handling bank cards to conform to numerous security standards regulated by Visa and MasterCard

Cost of Noncompliance

As if the requirements in the statutes themselves were not burdensome enough, many of the regulations include significant penalties for failing to comply with the data privacy statutes. A few of the legal penalties include:

- Up to *$750,000* in penalties *can be* assigned to the company for failure to notify affected individuals.
- *Penalties of $10,000 per violation* **can be** assigned to officers/directors personally (Gramm-Leach-Bliley Act);
- Fines of up to *$50,000 per violation* **can be** given for consumer health information retained on a hard drive (HIPAA).
- Officers/directors can serve *up to five years in prison*.
- Banks can *lose FDIC insurance*.
- Bank officers can be *barred from industry* under Gramm-Leach-Bliley Act.
- State privacy statutes provide for private civil actions for instances of noncompliance, including *punitive damages and attorneys' fees*. Under HIPAA, failure to properly erase consumer health information can carry a *minimum prison term of one year.*

A comprehensive approach to data privacy and network security is the most effective means to avoid a data breach and is the best way to be prepared to respond to a breach when necessary. It is important for organizations to recognize the need to be proactive. Complying with the latest data security laws through a comprehensive approach will provide benefits in the immediate future, reducing the likelihood of a data breach, and minimizing the loss when such an event occurs.

Part two in this series will feature various proactive steps organizations should take to be compliant with data privacy laws and regulations, including drafting and implementing appropriate data privacy policies and procedures and ongoing training of employees on the importance of data security. The article will also include a discussion of cyber-insurance coverage available to help insurers mitigate the cost of a breach and protect an organization's balance sheet.

The third part in the series will discuss the data breach response process and appropriate notifications to affected individuals and state attorneys general, in addition to media notice when necessary, public relations management and credit monitoring to help mitigate damages incurred.

References

1. Privacy Rights Clearinghouse, *Chronology of Data Breaches*, Available from: https://www.privacyrights.org/data-breach.
2. Verizon, *Data Breach Investigations Report, Available from:* http://www.verizonbusiness.com/Products/security/dbir/?CMP=DMC-SMB_Z_ZZ_ZZ_Z_TV_N_Z041.

ANATOMY OF A DATA BREACH, PART 2: PROACTIVE MEASURES AND REQUIREMENTS TO MINIMIZE THE RISK OF A DATA BREACH

James J. Giszczak, Dominic A. Paluzzi, and Kevin J. Pastoor

The average cost of a data breach is in the millions of dollars and penalties of up to $750,000 may be enforced for noncompliance. Unfortunately, it's not a matter of *whether* your organization will become a victim of a data breach but *when*.

There's a myriad of state, federal, and private data privacy regulations that, depending on the industry, a company must be compliant with. It's critical that an entity have a comprehensive approach to data privacy and network security to limit its risk and exposure with proactive measures and requirements to minimize the risk of a data breach.

Written Information Security Program

A written information security program (WISP) is a document that outlines an organization's privacy policies and procedures. The WISP name sounds much more daunting than the actual plan itself. Depending on the company and its complexity, the WISP can be fewer than ten pages. The WISP sets forth the various steps your company has taken to secure personal information (PI), protected health information (PHI), and confidential information contained in both electronic and hardcopy form.

A WISP is required to the extent an organization must comply with the Massachusetts Standards for the Protection of PI (201 CMR 17.00), Gramm-Leach-Bliley ACT (GLBA), and Federal Trade Commission (FTC) Red Flags Rule.

Massachusetts requires the following to be contained in a WISP:

- designation of at least one employee to maintain the program
- identification and assessment of reasonably foreseeable risks, and evaluation and improvement of current safeguards
- development of security policies for employees
- imposition of disciplinary measures for violations
- prevention of access to records by former employees
- taking all reasonable steps to verify that any third-party service providers with access to PI have the capacity to protect such PI in the manner provided for in this statute
- requiring third-party service providers by contract to implement and maintain appropriate security measures
- limitation of PI collected
- identification of paper, things, and media upon which PI is stored
- reasonable restrictions of access to PI

- regular monitoring
- review, at least annually, of security measures and
- documentation of responsive action

Should an organization suffer a data breach impacting a Massachusetts resident, or if this organization is governed by GLBA or FTC Red Flags Rule, it's almost a guarantee that an attorney general or other federal department will request to see the company's WISP, and the company had better have one to send immediately. Otherwise, fines and penalties will almost certainly dramatically rise.

Incident Response Plan

The incident response plan is the go-to document that identifies the appropriate internal and external resources to properly deal with a data breach. If an organization processes credit cards, it must comply with the Payment Card Industry Data Security Standards (PCI DSS). Among the many requirements within PCI DSS is the obligation to implement an incident response plan. Even if your organization does not necessarily need to comply with PCI DSS, an incident response plan is a critical component to proactive planning for data privacy compliance.

The incident response plan sets forth the incident response team, which is a group of decision makers (within and outside the organization) in legal, IT, risk management, human resources, marketing, and public relations. Compiling the incident response team today is essential, as a data breach impacts nearly every component of the business. Data breaches inevitably occur over holidays and weekends or after normal business hours. That's why it's important that all critical decision makers are listed in one place, with all contact information included. The incident response plan should include the appropriate vendors to contact (forensics, mail house, public relations firms). When a breach occurs there are many fast-moving parts, and it's critical all appropriate individuals on the incident response team are aware of their responsibilities. The incident response plan also sets forth the method and acceleration of communicating the incident both within the company and to the public (as necessary). It is also important to understand who is *not* part of the incident response team. This ensures the company is keeping the data breach incident on a need-to-know basis. Drafting the incident response plan and forming the incident response team upfront will greatly benefit your company when a data breach occurs (remember, it's not *whether* you'll suffer a data breach but *when*).

Confidentiality Agreements

An organization should set the tone from the beginning relative to their commitment to data privacy. Carefully drafted confidentiality agreements for employees, vendors, and visitors can accomplish this goal in part. Companies seem to do a decent job of having their employees sign an employment agreement that obligates the employee to keep trade secrets and intellectual property of the business confidential. But very few confidentiality agreements encompass an employee's obligation to keep PI and PHI confidential and a duty not to disclose such information. If in the employee's agreement you define what the business means by PI and PHI, it will be clear that your company takes privacy of such information seriously. Tie the nondisclosure of confidential information and intellectual property with PI and PHI as well. Also, an indemnification provision can be helpful in protecting an organization from an employee whose negligent or intentional acts result in a data breach. In that case, the company can look to the employee to recover losses incurred in having to notify affected individuals, attorneys general, and other state and federal agencies of the breach.

It is just as important to ensure that your company includes a similar confidentiality and indemnification provision in its contracts with vendors. In many instances, a data breach does not occur at the company but rather with one of its vendors. The breach notification statutes, however, require the company to notify the affected individuals and state and federal agencies since the company "owns" the PI. Having well-written confidentiality and indemnification provisions with your vendors will support your demand for any recoupment of costs from the vendor after the breach. Plus, if your business has any PI of a Massachusetts resident, you are required by statute to include, in all vendor contracts, a provision the vendor is in compliance with the Massachusetts standards for the protection of PI.

Finally, to the extent your business allows visitors access to its offices where PI may be viewed, it's critical you have such visitors sign a brief confidentiality acknowledgment. As a general rule, on the days visitors will be in your office, employees should remove all confidential and sensitive information from plain view, especially any documents containing PI or PHI.

Appropriate IT and Electronic Policies

Your company's data security and asset protection program is not complete with just a WISP, incident response plan, and confidentiality agreements. In today's electronic and social-networking world, employees are the largest threat to an organization's privacy and protection of PI and confidential information. A recent study by the Ponemon Institute, which surveyed 945 individuals who were laid off from, fired from, or quit their jobs in the past twelve months, 59 percent admitted to stealing company data.

A company can reduce the likelihood of a data breach resulting from the actions of one of its employees by having appropriate

IT and electronic policies as part of its data security and asset protection program. Such policies include

- social-media policy
- computer usage policies (cell phones, USBs, laptops, personal devices)
- document destruction policy
- electronic hardware/backup tape destruction policy
- e-mail retention policy and
- telecommuting policy

Of course, it's not enough that the company has the policies in place. Employees must actually receive the policies and have knowledge of their contents. For example, should an employee post a comment on Facebook that is harmful to the business or "tweet" (via Twitter) an individual's PI or PHI, the company must take immediate and appropriate action against that employee that is consistent with the company's IT and electronic policies.

Proper and Ongoing Training of Employees on the Company's Data Security Programs

The last thing any company wants to hear in a deposition of one of its employees after it has suffered a data breach is that the employee was not aware of any of the company's data security programs or policies. It is imperative employees are provided with appropriate training regarding the company's data security programs at the inception of employment. This training can be as simple as a ten-slide presentation on the company's policies and steps the organization takes to protect PI, PHI, and confidential information. Annual training is also a good idea to keep policies fresh in the minds of employees.

Should your company update any of its data security programs or policies, updated training would be appropriate at such time. After the employee watches the presentation or views the slides or attends a training session, have the employee sign an acknowledgment confirming his or her attendance and understanding of the company's data security programs and policies. This type of preventive measure will be important should the company suffer a data breach.

PI Storage and Disposal Laws

PI is often collected by organizations and is stored in various digital and paper formats. At least twenty-nine states have enacted laws that require entities to destroy, dispose, or otherwise make PI unreadable or undecipherable when such PI is no longer needed for a legitimate business purpose. Most of the statutes read, in part:

> A business shall take all reasonable steps to destroy or arrange for the destruction of a customer's records within its custody or control containing personal information that is no longer necessary to be retained by the business by shredding, erasing, or otherwise modifying the personal information in those records to make it unreadable or undecipherable.

As a result of these disposal statutes, the memories on old computers in the storage closet need to be properly erased and disposed of. Also, today's advanced copiers have a memory contained in their hard drive. Before that leased copier is returned, it's critical the copier's memory is erased of all PI and PHI. Failure to take these proactive steps can result in major fines and penalties for the company.

Cyber-Liability Insurance Coverage

Before you consider purchasing security and privacy insurance (a.k.a. network risk or cyber-liability insurance), you should contemplate a few issues. First, most entities have outsourced information, and you have to make sure third-party vendors are in compliance with your IT and data security procedures. You need a representation and warranty from the vendor stating its company is up to standards and will hold harmless and indemnify the company because it has your critical data. Second, you need to explore your existing insurance coverage. Look at your general liability, property, crime, and directors and officers policies. You may already have some level of coverage for breaches of data, data loss and media, and copyright and trademark issues.

Once you have reviewed your contracts with vendors and reviewed your current policies to determine the level of coverage that they provide, it is now time to consider purchasing a policy to address security and privacy risk and fill the gaps from your current policies.

As a rule of thumb, if you've seen one security and privacy policy . . . you've seen one security and privacy policy. Coverage forms can be dramatically different. Coverage can be purchased for third-party liability such as disclosure of employee PI or patient PHI via computer network or offline (paper records); invasion of privacy, defamation, libel, slander; intellectual property (infringement of copyright/trademark); or failure of computer network security and security or privacy breach regulatory proceedings. Security and privacy insurance is also available for first-party coverage such as business interruption—loss of income due to failure of network security; intangible property—costs to restore or recreate data or software resulting from failure of network security; forensic costs; ID Theft resources; and credit monitoring and costs associated with statutory notification requirements.

Security and privacy insurance coverage continues to evolve, so you need to work with a broker or agent who understands the coverage and takes the time to understand your company's unique situation.

If a company takes a proactive approach to data privacy compliance, it will minimize the risk of a data breach. Should a breach occur, the company will be in a much better position to quickly address the breach and curtail the losses to the affected individuals and the organization.

In addition to having appropriate data privacy policies and procedures and ongoing training of employees on the importance of data security, all organizations, big or small, private or public, should give serious consideration to purchasing cyber-liability insurance to help mitigate the cost of a breach and protect their balance sheet.

The third and final part in the series will discuss the data breach response process and appropriate notifications to affected individuals and state attorneys general, in addition to media notice when necessary, public relations management and credit monitoring to help mitigate damages incurred.

ANATOMY OF A DATA BREACH, PART 3: IMMEDIATE ACTION ITEMS UPON A DATA BREACH

James J. Giszczak and Dominic A. Paluzzi

Introduction

In a recent Ponemon Institute study, 62 percent of respondents indicated that a notification of a data breach decreased their trust and confidence in the organization, and 39 percent surveyed said they would consider ending the relationship with the organization. The study noted that properly communicating the circumstances of the data breach, however, can positively influence customer loyalty, trustworthiness, and reputation.

Typical Scenario

So here's the typical scenario. Mark, an account representative at a prominent staffing company (the hypothetical "XYZ Company") packs up from a long day at work and puts his laptop in the backseat of his car, along with an expandable folder with hundreds of human resources files from a new client. Mark then goes to the local diner to grab a quick bite to eat. When Mark leaves the restaurant to head home, he finds his car has been broken into. The missing radio, sunglasses and '80s CDs are not Mark's biggest problem. Rather, the loss of the HR files containing personal information (PI) and protected health information (PHI) will be the source of sleepless nights for Mark and XYZ's senior management. Mark's computer and the hard-copy files contained PI such as social security numbers, drivers' license numbers, banking records, passport numbers, credit-reporting histories, and PHI including medical information, treatment, diagnosis, and medical insurance information.

There are many moving pieces—so what should Mark and XYZ Company do next?

Gather the incident response team.

If you just read the above and are asking yourself, "What is an incident response team?" you are not alone. The Incident Response Team is a group of decision makers in legal, IT Risk, HR, marketing and public relations. The composition of the Incident Response Team is critical as a data breach impacts almost every component of the organization. The Incident Response Team will be predetermined and will be set forth in the Incident Response Plan which is the "go to" document that identifies the appropriate internal and external resources to properly deal with a data breach.

Call insurance agent.

Cyber-liability insurance is the newest coverage being offered by top brokers and agents around the world. Cyber-liability coverage can be complicated and may cover losses and expenses related to event management, cyber extortion, business interruption loss, fines and penalties, computer forensics, notices, network security liability, privacy liability, and electronic media liability coverage. The insurance agent must be put on notice at the very outset of the breach so that he or she is included in all relevant communications to ensure appropriate notice to the insurance carrier.

1. **Call experienced data privacy attorneys.**

   The incident response team, Mark, and others should not be e-mailing each other regarding the cause of the breach or potential exposure. All these e-mails could be discoverable in litigation or an investigation. It is critical an attorney with data security experience is immediately brought onboard to preserve the privilege of communications. This is not the time to call your corporate or estate-planning attorney. Having the wrong professional or inaccurate advice as to whether notice is required, who to notify, what to include in the notification, and when to send it can result in substantial (six- or seven-figure) penalties, fines, or judgments as a result of private rights of action and attorneys general enforcement actions.

2. **Determine and assign breach coordinator.**

   One individual from the incident response team must be selected to coordinate the breach response efforts internally and externally. This individual will be responsible for communicating with legal, HR, public relations, and outside vendors. It is critical the organization has a consistent message with regard to the incident and the steps the company is taking to notify the affected individuals and ensure PI and PHI in the company's possession is safeguarded in the future.

3. **Preserve evidence of breach and secure IT systems.**

   When a breach is discovered, it is important a forensics expert, either located within the company or an external vendor, is retained to contain the breach. In Mark's example, it's important to determine whether the computers were encrypted, what may have been on the laptop, whose PI and/or PHI may be threatened, and what was contained in the applications. Most importantly, IT needs to secure the systems to make certain a subsequent hacking incident does not take place, especially given the chance the thieves have the ability either to access the system themselves or sell the laptop and hardcopy PI on the black market to an expert who knows how to steal identities. It is critical to contain the damage.

4. **Contact law enforcement.**

Mark probably contacted the local police and filed a police report for the theft of his vehicle and laptop. (Counsel will most likely also be in touch with federal authorities regarding the incident.) Mark most likely did not mention, however, that the laptop and expandable folder contained PI and PHI of thousands of individuals. Most of the data breach notification statutes (which most of the states and provinces have each enacted various different versions of) allow for a delay in notification to affected individuals pending law-enforcement investigation.

5. **Breach notification letters: Do they need to be sent? Who gets them? When are they sent? What should they say? What should they not say?**

One of the most complicated components of the data breach process is the breach notification letters to affected individuals. This is most confusing due to the fact that most states and provinces have each enacted their own breach notification statutes that require notification based on different triggering events, such as when reasonable likelihood of harm to an individual exists, when the incident could result in identity theft, whether PI is subject to further unauthorized disclosure, when misuse of PI has occurred, or when the incident is likely to cause loss or injury or economic loss or financial harm.

The state/province of residence of the affected individual determines the applicable notification law. So a company that experiences a large data breach will most likely have to be compliant with almost every one of the breach notification laws, in addition to foreign notification laws.

Moreover, each of the statutes requires different elements in the breach notification letter. Some states/ provinces require the entity disclose the breach incident with specific detail, while other states, such as Massachusetts, prohibit any details of the breach be disclosed to affected individuals. Many of the laws also require notifications be sent by certain time periods (e.g., within forty-five days of discovery of the breach). Depending on the amount of notices, companies can either send the letters directly or work with a mail house to do so.

If the laptop was encrypted, XYZ Company may have dodged a huge bullet and may not have to provide notice, unless, of course, the encryption key is on a sticky note attached to the top of the laptop! It happens more often than you think!

6. **Offer credit monitoring.**

The credit-reporting agencies offer a credit monitoring service wherein they will monitor any suspicious behavior of a credit file and report same to the individual. Companies who experience data breaches will often provide, at no charge to the individual, a twelve-month credit monitoring subscription to the affected individuals. This serves at least two purposes: (1) it eases the individuals' minds that their identity will be monitored and not compromised without their knowledge; and (2) it mitigates the entities' damages should a negligence lawsuit be filed in the future against it.

7. **Draft press release.**

Depending on the number of individuals who must be notified and the type of information that was compromised, XYZ Company may be required to publish a press release or media statement with information about the breach. The press release may also appear on the company's website, and you must assume it will end up on other sites that track data breaches, such as www.datalossdb.org. As such, it is critical that experienced counsel is involved in this process as well.

8. **Draft FAQs.**

To assist with call-center operations and for consistent messaging, organizations should draft a Frequently Asked Questions (FAQs) document with answers to questions the organization will most likely receive from affected individuals, state agencies, and the press. FAQs are often posted to the company's website in an effort to streamline communication.

9. **Notify appropriate agencies.**

Many of the breach notification statutes require that entities notify state agencies, such as attorneys general, office of cyber security, and/or state police. In many instances the state agencies require full disclosure of the breach incident, the number of state residents affected, and a redacted copy of the notification letter.

If PHI was compromised, the office of Health and Human Services must also be notified under the Health Information Technology for Economic and Clinical Health (HITECH) Act. Notification to major state media outlets is also necessary under HITECH if more than five hundred people from one state were affected.

10. **Report incident to credit card companies and credit-reporting agencies.**

If credit card numbers were compromised in the incident, XYZ Company will most likely, by contract with Visa or MasterCard, have the obligation to notify the credit card companies. In addition, if the threshold number of affected individuals is met in any one state (e.g., one thousand for most states), the organization is required to notify the credit-reporting agencies of the breach incident.

It is not the case of *whether* a data breach will occur to an organization, but *when*. It is critical that organizations engage now in proactive measures to minimize the risk of a data breach and be prepared and take appropriate and immediate actions when a data breach does occur. The above action items are just a starting point. It's essential that organizations work with experts in the data privacy arena when preparing for and responding to a data breach.

MOBILE DEVICES AND DATA BREACH RISKS

Elizabeth Jonker

Nowadays, society has an ever-increasing reliance on mobile devices such as laptops, tablet computers, PDAs, USB drives, smartphones, and cell phones. These devices have infiltrated the workforce to improve communications and data management, make jobs easier, and keep us connected. The health-care industry is no exception. Great strides have been made to secure everything from e-mail to electronic health records. The introduction of mobile devices to this industry has made it easy and convenient for health-care workers, researchers, and others to transport information and keep it on hand. However, these devices, because of their portability, are also susceptible to loss and theft[1-6] In fact, the 2011 Ponemon report on patient privacy and data security reported 52 percent of data losses in health care were the result of loss or theft of mobile devices[7].

Similarly, the US Department of Health and Human Services' (HHS) Annual Report to Congress on Breaches of Unsecured Protected Health Information indicates they received reports of 56 breach incidents involving 500 or more individuals that were caused by theft of mobile devices (42 laptop computers, 14 portable electronic devices), which accounts for 27 percent of all large breaches reported in 2010[8].The HHS also received 23 reports of incidents related to the loss of portable electronic devices, which accounts for 11 percent of all large breaches reported in 2010[8].In 2009, of the 45 breaches involving 500 or more individuals reported to the HHS, 14 involved the loss or theft of laptops or portable electronic devices (31 percent)[8].The annual Identity Theft Resource Center Breach Reports for 2011 reported that 25, or 29 percent, of the 86 breaches they found in the medical/health-care sector involved mobile devices, and these breaches accounted for 51.8 percent of the records breached in this sector (1,932,331 of a total 3,732,071 records)[9,10].

The Threats to Personal Health Information

Rampant use and dependency on mobile devices has introduced a new threat to unwanted disclosure of personal information, including personal health information (PHI). Privacy breaches due to loss or theft of mobile devices can expose personal details about one or many individuals' health as a result of the data being unencrypted. This type of breach has the potential to negatively impact the lives of the individuals exposed by affecting their livelihood and personal and professional relationships. Such an event also greatly impacts the organization that caused the breach either with fines or other penalties.

Another major threat to stored PHI on mobile devices is unauthorized access to the device[6]. Unauthorized access could occur if adequate security measures have not been put into place, such as proper authentication requirements or the sharing of passwords and PINs. Forensics tools or other methods (e.g., "backdoors") can be used to bypass control mechanisms and recover data from a device as well.

Malicious software, or Malware, is another threat to stored PHI on mobile devices[6]. Malware can be contracted through Internet downloads, e-mail, instant messaging, and/or Bluetooth communications on mobile devices. Once the malware is downloaded to the device, it can be used to eavesdrop on user input, obtain stored information, and erase information from the device; among other inconveniences, it can pose as the device owner. Spam sent to a device through electronic communications can be used in "phishing" attempts in which attackers will try to obtain user information and passwords by directing users to fake websites that impersonate legitimate websites[6].

Electronic eavesdropping is a problem as an adversary could potentially obtain PHI through eavesdropping on user input and communications[6].This can be done through the use of software loaded to a device, through network access points (wireless networks are particularly vulnerable), or through surveillance methods such as those used by law enforcement. Electronic tracking could be implemented on a device without the users' knowledge[6].Custodians can make use of tracking services to track the location of employees' devices, which could be helpful in the event a device is lost or stolen. However, if used by an adversary with more malevolent motives, electronic tracking does pose a risk and could lead to theft and/or unauthorized access.

Server-resident data could be a threat to PHI used on mobile devices if the user is storing data on servers maintained by an outside party, such as in the use of cloud computing[6] In this case, the data housed on the external server could be breached by the company that maintains the server or by another party that may have or could gain access to the server. If a breach of PHI should occur due to any of these threats, it can result in serious legal and practical consequences for the data custodian with whom the information was entrusted as well as the employee or researcher.

Obligations of Researchers

In terms of privacy breaches, what role should a researcher hold in protecting PHI stored on mobile devices? Researchers have an ethical obligation to protect the confidentiality of personal information they hold about their subjects; this is according to the Tri-Council Policy Statement: Ethical Considerations for Research Involving Humans which provides the ethical guidelines for human research in Canada.PHI should be protected through the use of physical, administrative, and technical safeguards that are incorporated into their research plans[11]. Research ethics boards in Canada (REBs) are obligated to ensure researchers have planned for appropriate measures to safeguard PHI.

Following the Tri-Council's policy, the Canadian Institutes of Health Research (CIHR) has provided Best Practices for Protecting Privacy in Health Research[12].These guidelines are applicable to CIHR-funded research. They suggest researchers take a "risk assessment and management approach" to safeguarding research data based on the type of data, level of risk, and the impact of a breach[12]. Recommended security measures include organizational safeguards such as confidentiality agreements, access restrictions, policies and procedures; technological measures such as encryption, data de-identification, authentication measures for data access and audit trails; and physical security measures such as keeping computers and files in a secure area (without public access), surveillance, limiting the number of locations where the data will be stored, and protecting data from destruction by floods and fire[12].

In the United States, mobile devices used for health research purposes are regulated by the Food and Drug Administration (FDA), which regulates all clinical research. Currently, the FDA has a draft guidance out for comment concerning the regulation of "Mobile Medical Apps." [13]They define a mobile medical application as "a mobile app that meets the definition of 'device' in section

201(h) of the Federal Food, Drug, and Cosmetic Act (FD&C Act); and either

- is used as an accessory to a regulated medical device; or
- transforms a mobile platform into a regulated medical device."[13]

The intended use of the mobile application determines whether it meets the definition of a "device." Mobile devices, or mobile platforms as they're called, are defined as "commercial off-the-shelf (COTS) computing platforms, with or without wireless connectivity, that are handheld in nature."[13] A mobile application is then defined as "a software application that can be executed on a mobile platform, or a web-based software application that is tailored to a mobile platform but is executed on a server."[13] When a mobile application executed on a mobile platform transforms that platform into a medical device, it is considered a mobile medical app, and the device on which it is installed will be treated as a medical device under the proposed FDA regulation.

The FDA proposed in 2011 the regulation of mobile apps as medical devices rather than the mobile platforms themselves because it is the application that changes the mobile platform into a medical device. In and of themselves, mobile platforms are not considered medical devices unless they are manufactured and/ or marketed specifically for medical use. The FDA does not want to regulate the average mobile platform manufacturer.[14]In the proposed regulation, they state, "If it is possible to run mobile medical apps on 'BrandNamePhone,' but BrandNamePhone is not marketed by 'BrandNameCompany' with a medical device intended use, then BrandNameCompany would not be a medical device manufacturer." [13]Only if the platform is intended and marketed to be used as a medical device would it be regulated as such[13,14]

There are a few ways the FDA dictates when a mobile app can transform a mobile platform into a medical device:

1. "Mobile apps that are an extension of one or more medical device(s) by connecting to such device(s) for purposes of controlling the device(s) or displaying, storing, analyzing, or transmitting patient-specific medical device data."[13]
2. "Mobile apps that transform the mobile platform into a medical device by using attachments, display screens, or sensors or by including functionalities similar to those of currently regulated medical devices." [13]
3. "Mobile apps that allow the user to input patient-specific information and using formulae or processing algorithms-output a patient-specific result, diagnosis, or treatment recommendation to be used in clinical practice or to assist in making clinical decisions."[13]

Applications that fall under one of these definitions are considered medical devices and are regulated as such. Depending on the classification of the device (Class I—III), different regulatory requirements apply. The general requirements that apply to all classes include establishment registration and medical device listing, quality system regulation, labeling requirements, medical device reporting (of adverse events), premarket notification, reporting corrections and removals, and in some cases investigational device exemption for clinical studies of investigational devices. Quality system regulation (21 CFR Part 820) requires manufacturers to develop policies, procedures, and controls to ensure the systems they produce are safe and effective. This requires verification and validation of the mobile app and the platform on which it is used. Electronic records created or transmitted on the mobile devices are subjected to the FDA regulations under 21 CFR 11. This regulation requires procedures be put in place to "ensure the authenticity, integrity, and, when appropriate, the confidentiality of electronic records, and to ensure that the signer cannot readily repudiate the signed record as not genuine."[15]

Obligations for Health Information Custodians

In Canada, the Personal Information Protection and Electronic Documents Act (PIPEDA) [16]is the federal regulation that applies to personally identifying information (PII), including health information collected and used by private sector organizations. There also exists provincial legislation in some provinces aimed at safeguarding PII and PHI[16].For example, the Personal Health Information Protection Act (PHIPA) in Ontario regulates the collection, use, and disclosure of PHI[17].This act sets out the duties and obligations of health information custodians to safeguard personal health information. This includes a duty to establish information practices, to use the minimal amount of personal health information necessary, and to retain, transfer, and dispose of personal health information in a secure manner[1,17]. In terms of mobile devices, these duties are the key to ensuring that personal health information that is stored or transferred on such devices remains secure.

There are generally ten accepted principles of fair information practices, which include accountability, identifying purposes, consent, limiting collection, limiting use, disclosure and retention, accuracy, safeguards, openness, individual access, and recourse[18].

These principles are reflected in guidelines from such groups as National Institute of Science and Technology (NIST), COACH (Canada's Health Informatics Association), and Center for Democracy and Technology (CDT),[19-21] as well as in the legislation[16,17].

Accountability

In the simplest terms, accountability represents the responsibility that the organization has to protect the privacy of information, including appointing a privacy officer and developing privacy policies and procedures.

Identifying Purposes

Identifying purposes requires an organization to be open about why information is being collected, used or disclosed, how it will be used, and to identify any new uses for the information if they arise.

Consent

Consent requires individuals be given the option to opt-out of data collection, use, or disclosure. Some exceptions exist to the requirement for consent in the legislation. For example, in some cases PHI can be used for research purposes without prior consent, but the research must be approved by and monitored by a Canadian REB or US IRB.

Limiting Collection

Limiting collection ensures that only the minimum amount of information required for the specific purpose specified is collected. For example, a company may need to collect your name and address for a credit card payment, but asking for your height or weight would not be relevant, and that information should therefore not be collected.

Limiting Use, Disclosure, and Retention

Limiting use, disclosure, and retention means the use of the information will be limited to the purpose for which it was collected and data will not be shared with a third-party without specific authorization to do so. This principle also refers to limiting user access to the data to only required personnel. Access to parts of the data may be further restricted based on the role of the user (e.g., receptionist versus doctor).

Accuracy

Accuracy regards the quality and completeness of the data collected. Data should be validated and errors corrected to minimize the possibility of using incorrect information about an individual.

Safeguards

Safeguards are security measures put in place to protect the information from unauthorized access, as well as preparing a response for any incidents that may occur.

Openness

Organizations should make their information practices publicly available and easily understandable.

Individual Access

Individual access focuses on allowing individuals to access information about themselves that the organization has collected. For example, the Freedom of Information and Protection of Privacy

Act in Ontario explains the obligations that the government has in regards to allowing individuals' access to the information public bodies hold about them.

Recourse

Recourse is the process available for complaints to be filed by individuals and investigated by the organization. Appropriate measures must be taken to correct any practices that are deemed faulty or inadequate upon investigation[18].

Recommendations to Help Protect PHI on Mobile Devices

The Office of the Privacy Commissioner of Canada has released several fact sheets with tips on protecting personal information on mobile devices[22,23]. In keeping with the fair information practices outlined above, these tips stress accountability, limiting collection/ storage of PHI on devices, safeguards such as strong passwords, encryption, and antivirus and firewall protection, and using VPNs (virtual private networks) to transmit information[22,23]. In regard to mobile devices used in the context of health research, the Information and Privacy Commissioner of Ontario (IPC) has applied these information practices with specific recommendations for mobile devices such as laptop and tablet computers, USB drives, and PDAs[1].Because the main risks of storing and transporting personal health information on a mobile device are loss, theft, and unauthorized access, the focus is on how to reduce these risks and avoid a data breach.

Protecting personal health information stored on mobile devices begins first with a culture of privacy. In accordance with PHIPA, and in keeping with the information security practices outlined above, data custodians are required to develop information practices that conform to applicable legislation and set out the purpose for which information will be collected, used, stored, and disclosed, as well as outlining how it will be protected[1]. This includes policies and procedures regarding the storage and transportation of PHI on mobile devices. NIST and similar organizations also recommend the development of mobile device security policies as a first step to protecting data privacy[6]. In regard to the researchers who may be using PHI, the IPC recommends that they also be required to comply with the data custodians' policies and procedures by way of data security agreements or other contractual agreements[1].PHIPA also requires data custodians minimize the amount of PHI that they collect, use and disclose to the minimal amount reasonably required. If personally identifiable information is not required for the purpose, de-identified or aggregate information should be used. And storing de-identified or aggregate information on a mobile device reduces or eliminates the risk of a privacy breach if the device goes missing.

In terms of security, PHIPA requires custodians put safeguards in place to protect against theft, loss, and unauthorized use, modification, disclosure, and/or disposal. The IPC provides specific recommendations in terms of protecting PHI on mobile devices including avoiding storing or transporting PHI on mobile devices when possible, using strong passwords for access, and using strong encryption[1].

Limiting Storage and Transport of PHI

Storing and transporting unencrypted PHI on mobile devices should be avoided. Alternatives could include using de-identified or aggregate data, or accessing the data remotely via VPN so no PHI is kept on the device itself.

Encryption

If PHI must be stored or transported on a mobile device, the device or data should be encrypted. The IPC has released a fact sheet on strong encryption in health care[24]and one on encryption of mobile devices which specifically outline the types of encryption and standards recommended[5].For strong encryption, the generally accepted standard is FIPS 140-2 issued by the National Information Institute of Standards and Technology[24,25]. Of the algorithms that fall under this standard, the most commonly used is AES (advanced encryption standard). The strength of the version of AES used is based on key length. AES-128 is the minimum, but AES-192 and AES-256 are stronger[5,24].For mobile devices, the IPC recommends whole-disk encryption, or device encryption of portable storage devices like USB drives, as it encrypts the entire drive/device, protecting all information stored there. It is therefore the most secure option when storing or transporting PHI on mobile devices. However, users should keep in mind that when data files are transferred from a device with whole-disk encryption, they are no longer protected unless additional file encryption has been applied to files themselves[26].

Some devices, such as PDAs, may not allow whole-drive encryption. In this case, virtual disk encryption is recommended, which encrypts a file on an existing drive and treats this as a virtual disk. Virtual disk encryption is susceptible to problems such as the creation of unencrypted temporary files that could persist on the device. Folder or directory encryption is not recommended for PHI as it is not a sufficient option for securing this type of data. Data custodians can also implement an enterprise-encryption solution that encrypts all devices under the control of the custodian. This ensures errors are avoided by enabling custodians to enforce encryption standards on every device rather than leaving it up to the employee to select and implement encryption themselves. In the fact sheet "Encrypting Personal Health Information on Mobile Devices," the IPC provides an encryption checklist that outlines their recommendations. This is a quick and easy reference tool custodians and researchers can use to ensure they have taken the right steps to safeguard the PHI stored on mobile devices.

Strong Passwords

Strong passwords for access to mobile devices are also recommended by the IPC to protect PHI. A strong password is "usually characterized by no dictionary words; a combination of letters, numbers and symbols; and eight or more characters, with 14 or more being ideal."[1] It is also recommended that login passwords be different from passwords or keys used to access encrypted data. Passwords should be changed on a regular basis, and automatic lock-out should be implemented after a number of failed login attempts[1].

Research Ethics Oversight

In the research domain in Canada, REBs are the bodies responsible for the oversight of research. For a research project to be conducted, generally an REB review of the proposed research plan is required. Although under PHIPA, REB approval is only required for studies that use PHI without consent; sponsors, funding agencies, publishers, and data custodians generally require review of all proposed research plans[1,17].The research plan must outline the purpose of the study and the PHI, which is required for this purpose. The researcher is expected to follow the principle of data minimization and only collect or use the minimal amount of PHI necessary. In cases where identifiable information is not needed, de-identified or aggregate information must be used. As previously mentioned, the Tri-Council policy statement obligates REBs to ensure researchers have planned for appropriate measures to safeguard the information they will be collecting and/ or using[11].Researchers must exhibit that they have or can put into place adequate safeguards, including for any mobile devices that will be used in the study or for data storage or transport, before the REB will approve the research proposal. This could pose additional challenges for research that intends to collect data through the use of mobile devices by patients. Some common uses of mobile devices by research subjects are for patient diaries and patient-recorded outcomes[27].In the case of patients recording and transmitting data via mobile devices, researchers have less control over the use of and access to these devices. Patients must be provided with adequate information on how to secure their device and their communications, and the safeguards needed to ensure that others do not gain unauthorized access to their PHI. When possible, researchers should consider keeping audit trails for patient devices to track access and use.

Following are some items that have been recommended by various agencies and organizations to be considered when using or planning to use mobile devices in health research:

1. Remote access to PHI from mobile devices—no storage of PHI on devices[4,6,28]
2. Use a virtual private network to access/transfer data[6,22,23,29,30]
3. Authentication credentials (i.e. strong passwords)[1,2,6,29,30]
4. Automatic locking of device[2,3,6,22,23,29]
5. Disable networking capabilities on device when not needed[6,29,30]
6. Only store/transport de-identified data on mobile devices (to the extent possible)[1,3,6,21,23,29]
7. Encrypt devices[1,2,5,6,21-24,26,29,31]
    a. Whole-disk/device encryption[5]

    b.   Virtual-disk encryption[5]

    c.   Enterprise encryption[5]

8. Avoid the use of folder or directory encryption to protect PHI on mobile devices [5]

9. Remotely delete data from lost or stolen devices[2,6]

10. Ensure all data is removed prior to disposal of devices[6,22,23]

11. Audit devices and/or applications[2,6,13]

12. Add prevention and detection software to devices (e.g., antivirus software and firewalls)[6,22,23,29,30]

13. Enable audit trails that track access to PHI from mobile devices[2]

14. Training/education for users[1,6,23]

15. Agreements regarding use of mobile devices[2]

16. Devices should never be left unattended (e.g., in a car)[6,22,23,29]

17. Report loss or theft immediately[29]

To help implement these recommendations and guidelines regarding mobile device security, some more technical guides are available. As previously mentioned, the FIPS 140-2 encryption standards[25] are available from NIST. NIST also provides technical guides for encryption technologies for end user devices (http:// csrc.nist.gov/publications/nistpubs/800-111/SP800-111.pdf), for cell phone and PDA security (http:// csrc.nist.gov/publications/ nistpubs/800-124/SP800-124.pdf), for securing external devices for tele-work (http://csrc.nist.gov/publications/ nistpubs/800-114/ SP800-114.pdf), and guidelines for securing radio frequency identification systems that may be used with mobile devices (http://csrc.nist.gov/publications/nistpubs/800-98/SP800-98_ RFID-2007.pdf).

References

1. Information and Privacy Commissioner of Ontario and CHEO, *"Safeguarding Personal Health Information When Using Mobile Devices for Research Purposes,"* Information and Privacy Commissioner of Ontario, September 13, 2011.
2. Claudia Tessier, *"Moving Targets. Maximizing the Rewards and Minimizing the Risks of Mobile Devices,"* Journal of AHIMA 81, no. 4 (2010): 38-40.
3. Sandra Fischer, Thomas E. Stewart, Sangeeta Mehta, Randy Wax, and Stephen E. Lapinsky, *"Handheld computing in medicine,"* J Am Med Inform Assoc. 10, no. 2 (2003): 139-49.
4. Jennifer Prestigiacomo, *"Mobile Health Care Anywhere: A Proliferation of Mobile Devices Means Specific Wireless Challenges for Health Care Organizations,"* Healthc Inform 2011 no. 3 (Mar.28, 2011): 34, 36.
5. Ann Cavoukian, *"Encrypting Personal Health Information on Mobile Devices,"* Information and Privacy Commissioner of Ontario, May 2007.
6. Wayne Jansen and Karen Scarfone, *"Guidelines on Cell Phone and PDA Security,"* National Institute of Standards and Technology, US Department of Commerce, 2008.
7. Ponemon Institute LLC, *"Second Annual Benchmark Study on Patient Privacy and Data Security,"* Ponemon Institute, December 2011.
8. US Department of Health and Human Services, *"Annual Report to Congress on Breaches of Unsecured Protected Health Information for Calendar Years 2009 and 2010,"* US Department of Health and Human Services Office of Civil Rights, 2011.
9. Identity Theft Resource Center, *"ITRC Breach Stats Report,"* 2011, http://www.idtheftcenter.org/artman2/uploads/1/ITRC_Breach_Stats_Report_2011_20120207.pdf, Accessed on March 1, 2012.
10. Identity Theft Resource Center, *"Data on the Move Summary,"* 2011, http://www.idtheftcenter.org/artman2/uploads/1/Data_On_The_Move_Summary_20111231.pdf, Accessed on March 1, 2012.
11. Panel on Research Ethics, *"Tri-Council Policy Statement: Ethical Conduct for Research Involving Humans, 2nd edition,"* 2009.
12. Canadian Institutes of Health Research, *"CIHR Best Practices for Protecting Privacy in Health Research,"* 2005.
13. Food and Drug Administration *"Draft Guidance for Industry and Food and Drug Administration Staff: Mobile Medical Applications."* Food and Drug Administration (FDA), July 21, 2011.
14. Brian Dolan, *"FDA Drafts Mobile Medical App Regulations,"* Mobi Health News, July 19, 2011.

15. Code of Federal Regulations Title 21, Part 11.

16. Personal Information and Electronic Documents Act (PIPEDA), C5, 2000.

17. Personal Health Information Protection Act (Ontario), 2004.

18. Office of the Privacy Commissioner of Canada. *"Complying with the Personal Information Protection and Electronic Documents Act."* Office of the Privacy Commissioner of Canada, 2005.

19. CDT and Future of Privacy Forum. *"Best Practices for Mobile Applications Developers."* CDT and Future of Privacy Forum, 2011.

20. National Institute of Standards and Technology. *"Security and Privacy Controls for Federal Information Systems and Organizations: Information Security."* National Institute of Standards and Technology, US Department of Commerce, July 2011.

21. COACH. *"2011 COACH Guidelines for the Protection of Health Information,"* COACH, 2011.

22. Office of the Privacy Commissioner of Canada. *"Privacy on the Go: Ten Tips for Individuals on Protecting Personal Information on Mobile Devices."* Office of the Privacy Commissioner of Canada, January 2011.

23. Office of the Privacy Commissioner of Canada, *"Privacy on the Go: 10 workplace tips for protecting personal information on mobile devices."*

24. Office of the Privacy Commissioner of Canada, Jan-2011.24. Ann Cavoukian and Ross Fraser, *"Health-Care Requirement for Strong Encryption,"* Information and Privacy Commissioner of Ontario, July 2010.

25. National Institute of Standards and Technology, *"Security Requirements for Cryptographic Modules" (FIPS PUB 140-2)*, National Institute of Standards and Technology, US Department of Commerce, 2001.

26. Karen Scarfone, Murugiah Souppaya, and Matt Sexton, *"Guide to Storage Encryption Technologies for End-User Devices,"* National Institute of Standards and Technology, US Department of Commerce, 2007.

27. AndreasKoop and RalphMosges. *"The Use of Handheld Computers in Clinical Trials,"* Control Clin Trials 23, no. 5 (2002): 469-80.

28. RajGururajan, *"A Study of the Use of Hand-Held Devices in an Emergency Department,"* J Telemed Telecare 10, no. Suppl 1 (2004): 33-5.

29. Ann Cavoukian, *"Safeguarding Privacy in a Mobile Workplace,"* Information and Privacy Commissioner of Ontario, June 14, 2007.

30. Karen Scarfone and Murugiah Souppaya, *"User's Guide to Securing External Devices for Tele-work and Remote Access."* National Institute of Standards and Technology, US Department of Commerce, 2007.

31. Daniel C. Baumgart, *"Personal Digital Assistants in Health Care: Experienced Clinicians in the Palm of Your Hand?"* Lancet 366, no. 9492 (2005): 1210-22.

SECTION III

Health Information Privacy

IT TAKES A VILLAGE TO PROTECT PERSONAL HEALTH INFORMATION

Rebecca Herold

In a novel twist on the axiom that "it takes a village to raise a child," North America's emerging privacy and security infrastructure is rapidly realizing that a coordinated community effort is needed to safeguard personal health information. There is no single "silver bullet" for effectively securing information; you need to implement layers of security to successfully safeguard information.

Just because one type of safeguard does not provide total security does not mean you shouldn't use it. For example, consider the effective and commonly used security tool, encryption. It would be silly to not use encryption simply because it does not provide complete security for the encrypted data; you will always have risks related to human error, malicious intent, vulnerable system designs, and poorly implemented or buggy encryption that will leave the data less than 100 percent secure. For example, those using encryption sometimes write the encryption password down and store it with the data storage device. This was recently demonstrated when a UCLA Health System doctor's laptop was stolen from his home, along with the piece of paper containing the encryption password. Human failings defeated encryption, not the technology itself. Encryption should still be used along with other controls and defenses, such as access controls, logging, training, and enforced policies, just to name a few, to help to make up for the inherent shortcomings. The same is true for privacy; there is not a simple single action you can take or tool you can use to effectively preserve 100 percent privacy. Layers of privacy controls need to be established to get to an acceptable level of privacy assurance.

One valuable privacy tool is de-identification, a process used to make personal information anonymous, or at least as anonymous as possible. Leaders throughout the world are recognizing de-identification as a good privacy tool that, when used appropriately, can advance many types of research activities. For example, on December 5, 2011, UK Prime Minister Cameron lauded the use of de-identification when he was quoted by the BBC as saying, "Let me be clear, this does not threaten privacy, it doesn't mean anyone can look at your health records, but it does mean using anonymous data to make new medical breakthroughs. The end result will be that every willing patient is a research patient and every time you use the NHS you are playing a part in the fight against disease at home and around the world."[1]

Other leaders in other countries have also encouraged the use of de-identification as an effective privacy practice when used with other controls. In a paper released in the summer of 2011, Ontario's Information and Privacy Commissioner Dr. Ann Cavoukian recommended the use of de-identification as an effective tool to protect privacy to the benefit of individuals and society in general when she wrote in the press release, "Not only does de-identification protect individual privacy, it also enables the valuable use of information for authorized secondary purposes, such as health research."

Consider also that the US government established the acceptance of de-identification within the Health Insurance Portability and Accountability Act (HIPAA) by indicating that de-identified protected health information (PHI) could generally be used for research purposes.

Simply put, the goal of de-identification is to remove only as much personally identifiable information items as necessary so the data cannot reasonably be tied to a specific individual. The amount of nonreversible de-identification—re-identification risk—should correlate with the purposes for which the data was de-identified; and the entities that will have access to the de-identified data. These issues will all determine the additional safeguards organizations will need to effectively protect privacy.

I know some privacy advocates and researchers have been vocal in their criticism of de-identification methods, and I've heard some say it shouldn't be used at all as a privacy control. While I certainly respect their work, my concern is that their findings narrowly examine the merits of de-identification. What I have not seen factored in is the impact of risk assessments of all the parties involved in data sharing and the effective use of additional safeguards, as should be detailed within data-sharing agreements. However, I continue my search for research that goes beyond the single de-identification action to assess the effectiveness of de-identification in conjunction with other security controls and risk mitigation methods. While de-identification may not be a perfect science, it certainly is still a good and feasible option that has been shown to effectively reduce breaches while releasing the optimal amount of data.

Let's consider some facts specific to health care:

- More patient records are being digitized as electronic health records (EHRs) or electronic medical records (EMRs) than ever before.

- More privacy breaches involving patient information are occurring than ever before.
- As our population becomes greater in numbers and older, more health problems, illnesses, and diseases are being diagnosed and treated than ever before.

With this massive amount of ever-growing digital medical data, there is a great opportunity to use new research technologies to more effectively and efficiently treat, and even find cures for, the vast array of medical problems if we can securely de-identify the data. When coupled with other safeguards, de-identification can provide an excellent strategy for organizations seeking to leverage vast amounts of personal information to benefit research, and the technology has earned a rare few criticisms from the general public. In the BBC News article, an opponent to the currently-planned use of de-identified patient records for research (with no patient consent) expressed concern that the provision of "medical data including postcodes and age profiles would permit private firms the ability to trace back to the individuals concerned."

Admittedly, if risk thresholds are not supported by professional guidance and the accompanying safeguards, the risk of re-identification increases. Re-identification can be measured and data would only be shared if that risk was acceptably low. However, a blanket statement that de-identification on its own is not 100 percent nonreversible and therefore should not be trusted would be akin to saying that simply using seatbelts alone does not keep 100 percent of vehicle passengers from being hurt or killed, so seatbelts shouldn't be used. Doesn't this seem a bit silly? Well, it does now, but early on, when seatbelts were introduced most people didn't want to use them. History has shown the effectiveness of seatbelts. Of course you want to use seatbelts, along with airbags, keeping doors shut, having properly working brakes, and so on, to help reduce the harms that could occur in car accidents. Likewise, de-identification should be used along with other safeguards to reduce the privacy risks. As the volumes of personal health data continue to expand and innovative new methods are devised to harness the information, I'm confident history will also show that de-identification is an effective privacy tool.

Relevant Reading

1. "Everyone 'to be Research Patient', Says David Cameron" *BBC NewsUK Politics*, http://www.bbc.co.uk/news/uk-16026827, accessed December 13, 2011,
2. Ann Cavoukian and Khaled El Emam, "Dispelling the Myths Surrounding De-identification: Anonymization Remains a Strong Tool for Protecting Privacy,". http://www.ipc.on.ca/images/Resources/anonymization.pdf, June 2011.

THE USE OF PERSONAL HEALTH INFORMATION FOR RESEARCH PURPOSES IN CANADA: IT'S TIME TO COORDINATE THE CONVERSATION

Anita Fineberg

On March 14, 2012, Colin Hansen, the Liberal MLA for Vancouver-Quilchena and former health minister of BC wrote an op-ed article in the *Vancouver Sun* titled "Unlocking our Data to Save Lives: Analyzing Existing Electronic Health Care Records Could Help BC Residents and Save the Province Billions in Costs." Mr. Hansen notes, "It is time we proactively opened this B.C. advantage to health researchers and research funders locally, nationally and internationally. Not only would a more open-door policy bring in millions of new research dollars and human talent, it would lead to discoveries that will save more lives, improve quality of life and cement British Columbia as a centre of excellence for bringing efficient/effective health care solutions to the world."

I couldn't agree more. In fact, not only does this "treasure trove" of data exist in BC, each of the provinces, to a greater or lesser degree has vast amounts of data that could be "unlocked to save lives."

As far as patient privacy is concerned, Mr. Hansen writes that "we have laws and systems in place that make sure privacy is protected by removing personal identifiers. Researchers have no way of tracing the data they receive back to individual citizens."

There is certainly great interest in understanding how these privacy laws apply to personal health information to be used for research purposes across the country. The first webinar in which I addressed the privacy requirements in Ontario attracted the largest number of participants for an Electronic Health Information Laboratory webinar.[1] Part II in the webinar series closely examined the privacy requirements in BC and Alberta.[2]

However, I would suggest Mr. Hansen misses the point with his rather glib reference to the laws in place to protect patient privacy. First, research in Canada may be conducted using information that identifies an individual. All privacy legislation allows such information to be used as long as the research project has been granted research ethics board (REB) approval and meets varying criteria across the country. But secondly—and herein lies the rub—with ten Canadian provinces and the federal government having enacted privacy laws of either general or specific health-sector application, it is a major challenge for researchers to access the data in a timely, cost-effective, and coordinated manner.

Let's take Mr. Hansen's home province of BC as an example. Unlike some provinces, such as Ontario and Alberta, BC does not have privacy laws specifically applicable to personal health information. Health information in hospitals is subject to the public sector legislation, the Freedom of Information and Protection of Privacy Act (FOIPA), while information under the custodianship of the private sector, including physicians and pharmacies, is subject to the private sector legislation, the Personal Information Protection Act (PIPA). Finally, the E-Health (Personal Health Information Access and Protection of Privacy) Act (EPHIPA) regulates personal health information held in designated "health information banks," generally electronic databases of such information. So that's three different pieces of legislation in one province alone in which researchers must comply to access data for health research.

And lest we forget, it was only last November when FOIPA was amended to permit the disclosure of personal information outside of the country for research purposes that Mr. Hansen's call to proactively open BC health data to international researchers was legally permissible.

By my count, there are about nineteen different Canadian privacy laws applicable to the disclosure of personal or personal health information for research purposes. Some require provincial health ministry approval prior to access being granted to the data; REB approval is a precondition in others. Some, like the BC EPHIPA, mandate that application be made to a data stewardship committee. And all, speaking from more than twenty years of practice in the area, take time, effort, money, and a lot of patience before one even begins the negotiation of the agreement to establish the terms and conditions under which the data may be accessed and used. None are particularly user-friendly or easy to understand, even for those of us who have practiced in the area.

So while I'm cheering for Mr. Hansen from the sidelines, I'd suggest we first need a little more coordinated conversation across the country—to develop standard criteria for accessing the data, de-identification where possible, as well as reciprocity among research ethics boards, even within the same province, to avoid replication of research applications.

I'd also remind governments they do not "own" these treasure troves of data—they hold them in trust for the citizens of the country who were required to make it available in return for government services. In my opinion, governments are only the stewards of our data. Sure, in a publicly funded health system (a discussion for another day), the government as insurer needs such information to ensure the services have been performed and providers have properly submitted their claims for service delivery. But as data stewards, don't they also have an obligation to do more? To make the data available for the public good? For health research, public health surveillance studies, system utilization, and efficiency purposes, to name but a few, I say so. Such uses of the data would be win-win as they will also provide valuable insights into issues related to the more appropriate allocation of increasingly scarce health-care resources. But let's not assume that governments have the resources to do such work internally—they don't, nor should they. They are not in the business of conducting health research or analytics. Leave this to the experts!

Privacy legislation allows for the use of health information for these purposes, so let's not point the fingers at the lawyers this time. The issue is not that individual privacy is at risk; controls are in place. We've seen that the problem is, there exist too many disparate controls and practical barriers. Let's take another recent example from BC. The data linking amendments made to FOIPA in the fall of 2011 do not apply to the health sector. Commissioner Denham, the Information and Privacy Commissioner of British Columbia, responded to this exclusion by suggesting the possible need for stand-alone health information privacy legislation to address the "unique needs within the sector." I agree. Such legislation could at minimum, as is the case in provinces such as Ontario, New Brunswick, and Newfoundland, consolidate all the rules and streamline the processes for accessing information for health research from all sources—government-held databases, including electronic health records, and the private sector (assuming that such legislation was substantially similar to PIPEDA).

Mr. Hansen's first step should be to speak with the bureaucrats who hold the key to the treasure chest.

References

1. Electronic Health Information Laboratory Webinar, *"The Use of Personal Health Information for Research: A Tale of Three Provinces,"* Anita Fineberg, LL.B., CIPP/C, Anita Fineberg and Associates https://www.ehealthinformation.ca/survey/webinarfeb01122012.aspx, Recorded on February 1, 2012

2. Electronic Health Information Laboratory Webinar, *"The Use of Personal Information for Research: A Tale of Three Provinces Part II,"* Anita Fineberg, LL.B., CIPP/C, Anita Fineberg and Associates https://www.ehealthinformation.ca/survey/webinarapr042012.aspx, Recorded April 4, 2012

SO YOU'VE CONCLUDED YOUR NEW HEALTH START-UP IS OUTSIDE HIPAA—NOW WHAT?

Ann B. Waldo

Pop Quiz: True or False: If a US company handling health data isn't subject to HIPAA rules and regulations, it need not worry about privacy laws.

Answer: a resounding *false*!

One occasionally hears people from the HIPAA-regulated world opine that "outside HIPAA, it's the Wild West—no laws apply." Ill-thought-out policy recommendations sometimes follow from that wildly inaccurate assumption. Leaving policy matters for another day, the purpose of this article is to give someone designing a novel app or service involving consumer health information a sense of what their legal responsibilities actually are. It may surprise you to learn that a multitude of US federal and state obligations attach to you when you handle health information, even if you are completely outside the rules of HIPAA So if you think your new health tech endeavor is not subject to HIPAA regulations, what should you consider?

First and foremost, carefully test your assumption that you are outside HIPAA's regulations. The scope of HIPAA is not intuitive; HIPAA covers exactly what it covers, no more, no less. In nontechnical terms, HIPAA applies to "covered entities," which are health plans, health-care providers, and clearinghouses (if you have to ask what a clearinghouse is, you aren't one), and their "business associates," which are, in short, their vendors that access protected health information. Caution—these are terms of art with precise meanings. In fact, the new omnibus HITECH Rule has added further complexity to the analysis of what entities are considered business associates. If you have the slightest uncertainty about whether your entity is subject to HIPAA, seek counsel, for the consequences of mistakenly thinking the intricate requirements of HIPAA don't apply to you could be devastating.

Second, if you've definitively concluded HIPAA does not apply to you, which laws do?

Federal Trade Commission Law. The overarching law is regarding section 5 of the FTC Act, which bans businesses from engaging in unfair or deceptive acts affecting commerce. While this may sound vague, a long line of consumer protection case law and settlement decrees clarify what deceptiveness and unfairness mean. Not honoring one's privacy statement promises can be a misrepresentation under section 5. But lest you think that you could avoid that snare by having no privacy statement and making no promises, know that the FTC has closed that door—having inadequate security for personal identifiable information (PII) can be an "unfair" business practice, even if no promises whatsoever about security or privacy were made.

The FTC Has Made Its Commitment to Enforcing Consumer Privacy Protections Crystal-Clear. It has taken almost 150 privacy enforcement actions to final settlement decrees and has conducted an unknown number of additional investigations. The agency has released numerous resources explaining the legal obligations of companies to adequately collect, protect, handle, and dispose of personal information.

Because your new venture will involve health data, you should know that the bar is higher than for other PII, since the FTC classifies health data as "sensitive." The agency's 2012 privacy report[1] explains that sensitive data merits extra protection because of the greater potential for harm if misused. Incorporating proper protections for sensitive data as you craft your business model (which the FTC calls "privacy by design") requires careful planning and customization beyond the scope of this article. But one element to consider thoughtfully is the role of *consent*. For example, the FTC report states that if a health website is designed to target people with particular medical conditions, the site should seek affirmative express consent before marketing to them. The nature of the consent matters also, for the FTC expects certain types of consent to be clear and visible at a time when consumers are making a decision, not buried in separate legal documents.

Protecting the Security of Your Customers' Health Data Is a Serious Legal Obligation under the FTC Act. In FTC consent agreements, the agency regularly requires a "comprehensive, written information security plan." Although the FTC's security requirements are not as prescriptive and detailed as the HIPAA Security Rule is, FTC consent decrees have become more detailed regarding the requisite components of security plans. For example, note the security requirements in a recent FTC consent order against Compete, Inc.[2]. Unquestionably, your health venture thus must build in serious, comprehensive security safeguards before you take in that first customer's health information—and you'll probably need outside help building your security program. Even if you've concluded definitively that you are not subject to HIPAA, it might still be wise to build to the HIPAA Security Rule framework, not only because it is broadly recognized, but also because if your business model changes and you later integrate your product with a HIPAA-regulated entity, you'll already have that important security work done and documented in a HIPAA-compatible way.

Other Federal Laws. You have to do more than ensure you meet the high bar of the FTC Act. You should also be aware of FTC expectations and best practices regarding Fair Information Privacy Principles. Other federal privacy laws to evaluate include CAN-SPAM (e-mail marketing); COPPA (for websites targeting kids or knowingly accepting information from kids); the Do-Not-Call Registry; the Disposal Rule (for consumer reporting data); and the Red Flags Rule (measures to prevent identity theft). Additional privacy laws apply to credit-reporting agencies and financial institutions. Finally, if you are a personal health record vendor, or a vendor to such a vendor, you're subject to a uniquely applicable PHR breach notice law—check the definitions carefully to see if they apply to you.

State Consumer Protection Laws. State laws can and do pile on to the complex federal privacy requirements, and state Attorneys General (AGs) have not been shy about enforcing their laws. For starters, all fifty states have "little FTC Acts" that ban misrepresentation and unfair business practices affecting consumers. These laws give AGs essentially the same powers as the FTC, and sometimes even broader powers—for example, the state laws apply to nonprofit organizations. When a company is accused of a privacy violation, it is not unusual for state AGs to bring enforcement actions *in addition to the FTC's action*. Defending against multiple authorities is tough—and expensive.

State Breach Notice Laws. Almost all states require notices to be sent to consumers and government agencies when the security of certain consumer information is breached. Most of these laws are triggered by data useful for identity theft (such as credit card, bank account, social security, driver's license, and passport numbers). *However, health information triggers at least half a dozen breach notice laws.* This means that if you suffer a security breach (lost laptop, hacking, etc.) that compromises identifiable health information, you must immediately comply with the stringent notice requirements of a handful of state laws or face serious penalties.

State-Unique Privacy Laws. States have passed numerous information security, encryption, and social security number laws. Most aren't hard to comply with if you're already meeting the tough standards of overall consumer privacy laws. But one crucial law to note is the California Online Privacy Protection Act. This law requires websites interacting with California residents to have a privacy statement meeting certain requirements. Although enacted in 2003, the law is triggering dramatic new attention. *The California AG recently announced that she intends to impose fines of up to $2500 per download against mobile apps lacking compliant privacy statements*[3]. That means that if an app like Angry Birds failed to have a compliant privacy notice, its fine could be $2.5 trillion—enough to pay off the last couple years of the federal deficit!

State-Unique Medical Privacy Laws. A few states, including California, have comprehensive health privacy laws whose scope is much broader than HIPAA's, so you should evaluate whether the expansive definitions in such laws pull you in and trigger a host of obligations. In addition, almost all states have unique medical privacy laws applicable to certain conditions like HIV, other infectious diseases, reproductive health, mental health, genetic conditions, etc. These laws may or may not apply to your business model, but if they do, researching and applying them is extremely challenging. The situation gets even more complicated with respect to health information of teenagers, for whether the teen or the parent is the one permitted to access health information generally depends on whether the teen or the parent is the one empowered by state law to consent to treatment. For example, in one state, a fourteen-year-old girl can obtain gynecological care without her parents' knowledge, and it is thus *illegal* for the doctor to share any of the related medical records with the parent, whereas in the adjoining state, *not* sharing medical records with a parent in the same situation may be illegal. These inconsistencies pose enormous design challenges for national online health technology services. While some work-around solutions exist, much work is needed to ease this compliance burden on HIT innovation.

Anonymization and De-identification. Readers of *Risky Business* are familiar with the requirements of HIPAA de-identification and no doubt are aware that if only de-identified data is involved in a data breach, no breach reporting is required by HIPAA. Inside the HIPAA world, therefore, proper de-identification is critical. Outside HIPAA, there's no equivalent standard of what anonymization means, which is why loosely anonymized consumer

Anonymization According to the Federal Trade Commission and De-identified Consumer Data

The FTC recommends that de-identified data fall *outside* its proposed consumer framework if:

(1) a given data set is not reasonably identifiable;
(2) the company publicly commits not to re-identify it; and
(3) the company requires any downstream users of the data to keep it in de-identified form.[5]

data has been the subject of successful re-identification attacks, as in the Netflix case.[4] However, that doesn't mean that if you hold health data not regulated by HIPAA, you should feel free to casually redact obvious identifiers, declare it anonymous, and then do with it whatever you please. The FTC Report proposed a new three-part test for when data is sufficiently anonymized to no longer be subjected to the FTC's proposed framework for PII. If your business plans involve use of anonymized data, you should, at a minimum, carefully study the FTC's new anonymization guidance.

For maximum business flexibility, you may opt to anonymize your data to a level that would meet HIPAA de-identification standards.

Takeaway Messages. By now, it's clear that the notion that health data outside HIPAA is unregulated is absurd. Instead, baking privacy into a business involving health data requires complex decision making and awareness of the laws mentioned here. To cut through the legal complexities, I offer a few maxims:

- Say what you do (give clear notice up front).
- Do what you say (honor all your promises, including by building back-end processes to ensure you'll honor them).
- Realize that context matters enormously. What one person would welcome, another would find embarrassing or offensive. Build in meaningful choice wherever consent is required or reasonably expected.
- Don't surprise your users. If an action of yours may surprise or antagonize a reasonable user, don't do it—or ask for specific permission.
- Don't try to trap your users—let them (and their data) depart as they choose.
- Above all, safeguard their information. Protect their health data as though they had entrusted you to protect their cash.

References

1. Federal Trade Commissioner, *Protecting Consumer Privacy in an Era of Rapid Change: Recommendations for business and policy makers.* Available from: http://www.ftc.gov/opa/2012/03/privacyframework.shtm, 2012.
2. Federal Trade Commission, Compete, Inc. Consent Order, http://www.ftc.gov/os/caselist/1023155/121022competeincagreeorder.pdf
3. ArsTechnica, "CA to app devs: get privacy policies or risk $2500-per-download fines," http://arstechnica.com/tech-policy/2012/12/ca-to-app-devs-get-privacy-policies-or-risk-2500-per-download-fines/, December 4, 2012

4. Khaled El Emam, Elizabeth.Jonker, Luk Arbuckle, BradleyMalin, A Systematic Review of Re-Identification Attacks on Health Data, Accessed PLOSONE, http://www.plosone.org/article/info%3Adoi%2F10.1371%2Fjournal.pone.0028071, December 2,2011

5. Federal Trade Commission, *Protecting Consumer Privacy in an Era of Rapid Change*, http://www.ftc.gov/os/2012/03/120326privacyreport.pdf, March 2012

THE SECRET TO A LONG AND HEALTHY RELATIONSHIP WITH YOUR HEALTH-CARE PROVIDER

Jay Innes

Two recent patient surveys indicate that it is not just the rich and famous that worries about the security and confidentiality of personal health records. Patients are starting to ask questions about the migration to electronic health records (EHRs), and the questions may have an impact on the sacred doctor-patient relationship.

In 2011, the National Partnership for Women and Families and Alan Westin, professor emeritus, Columbia University, conducted a survey of more than 1,900 American adults to produce *Making It Meaningful: How Consumers Value and Trust Health IT*. The survey revealed that more than 80 percent of respondents do not feel they are adequately informed of the ways in which their medical information is collected and used. The study concludes that the onus falls on the physicians as the frontline caregivers to provide crucial guidance and that the physicians should "cultivate trust in EHRs."

In a webinar cosponsored by the company Privacy Analytics, health-care lawyer Ken Rashbaum reminded the attendees of a quote from Leon Rodriguez, when the director of the Office for Civil Rights (OCR) connected trust and health care, "If people lose trust in the healthcare system, they will not get the care they need." Rodriguez went on to tell the *Detroit Free Press* that "enforcement promotes compliance."

Rashbaum, who was providing information on the HIPAA spot audits in 2012 in the United States and advising on breach prevention strategies, acknowledges that this is an exciting but unsettled time for health-care sectors. As health-care providers in many countries move from paper to digital records encouraged by government incentives, patients are seeing the elevation of the roles of data stewards and IT departments.

"For the first time in medical history information has become a tool of care because we have the ability to coordinate and consolidate information from so many different sources," says Rashbaum, a New York attorney who has more than twenty-five years' experience in the health-care and pharmaceutical industries.

The report from the National Partnership for Women and Families goes on to highlight the fact that consumer education is needed to enhance the understanding of the link between the care process and the records systems that support care. Almost two-thirds of all respondents indicated that widespread adoption of EHRs will lead to the theft or loss of personal information, which, as Rashbaum indicates, strikes at the core of the bond of trust between the doctor and patient. "If patients lose confidence in the security and the trust in the confidentiality of their information then they are not going to be as forthcoming with their physicians and the information may no longer be reliable from the care point of view."

Rashbaum is quick to point out that the loss of confidence is less with the physicians than the mutable nature of electronic information (easier to lose than paper), and such concerns are exacerbated by media coverage of information leaks and losses that could potentially undermine the many beneficial uses for the electronic records. "If the data can't be trusted by the patient, then the patient will be reluctant to give full and comprehensive information, and then the physician may in turn look with less trust on the information," warns Rashbaum.

The reactions of patients who are concerned about the security of their records and the impact on trust were revealed in a recent four-country survey conducted for the Florida company FairWarning. The results measured patient expectations, actions, and reactions to concerns over the security of personal health records signaling an increase in public awareness. The surveys of patients in the United States, the United Kingdom, France, and Canada indicate that patients will alter behavior if trust is compromised and, in some instances, withhold information from health-care providers, which could be detrimental to future care strategies and treatments. The decision to withhold information from a care provider resulting in an inaccurate or incomplete health record may seriously harm the patient and diminish faith in the system, two reasons explaining the increased focus on enforcement.

In the survey summary of all four countries, more than 90 percent of patients responded that care providers have an ethical and legal obligation to protect privacy. Further emphasizing the relationship between doctor and patient, more than 85 percent of all respondents indicated that if they had a sensitive medical condition, the care provider's reputation would have an impact on the choice of provider. The four country surveys also indicate that patients will seek to impose consequences on the health-care executives who are responsible for a data breach.

"In every market the patient still has this trust with the care provider but they react very emotionally when things go wrong, all the way to the sacking of the executives," says Kurt Long, FairWarning CEO, admitting his surprise at the 90 percent response rate demanding fines or dismissal for executives who fail to act following a breach. "We conclude that there's a lot of trust and a belief that care providers are doing the right things but when it goes wrong, boy are they mad," adds Long.

With time to absorb the survey results and a commitment to use the current surveys to benchmark follow-up studies in the four countries, Long predicts a blend in openness and privacy in the future. "I think there is going to be this bifurcation and there will be a set of people who are comfortable with an awful lot of information about themselves being public. On the other hand, I think that there's going to be a core set of information, including our medical information—the most sensitive aspects of our medical conditions—that all of us are going to really value and want to protect."

Relevant Reading

1. National Partnership for Woman and Families and Alan Westin, *"Making It Meaningful: How Consumers Value and Trust Health IT,"* http://www.nationalpartnership.org/site/DocServer/HIT_Making_IT_Meaningful_National_Partnership_February_2.pdf?docID=9783 February 2012.

2. Electronic Health Information Laboratory, *"HIPAA Security Spot Audits Begin: Chicken Littles and Annual Traditions,"* Ken Rashbaum, Webinar for Privacy Analytics, https://www.ehealthinformation.ca/survey/webinarfeb132012.aspx, February 2012.

3. New London Consulting for FairWarning, *"How Privacy Considerations Drive Patient Decisions and Impact Patient Care Outcomes: Trust in the Confidentiality of Medical Records Influences When, Where, Who and What Kind of Medical Treatment Is Delivered to Patients,"* http://www.fairwarning.com/subpages/resources.asp#patientsurveys,2012.

4. Accenture, "Connected Health: The Drive to Integrated Healthcare Delivery," http://www.accenture.com/us-en/Pages/insight-making-case-connected-health.aspx?amp&sf3179485=1, 2012.

SECTION IV

Data De-identification
and Data Masking

WHAT IS ACCEPTABLE RE-IDENTIFICATION RISK?

Khaled El Emam

A number of academic and commercial organizations we have been working with recently asked about acceptable levels of re-identification risk as it pertains to using the statistical method to de-identify sensitive data. Determining an appropriate threshold is not only a key element of using the statistical method, it is one of the biggest challenges statisticians and disclosure-control experts face. The reason it is so important is that the threshold represents the maximum allowed re-identification risk in a database, in order for that database to not be considered personal health information.

When discussing this issue and what the current standard for de-identifying health information should be, the number that often comes up is a 0.04 percent re-identification risk threshold.

In this article I will first explain where that number (0.04 percent) comes from and what it means. Then I will provide a detailed analysis of why organizations should not use that number as a threshold, closing with some recommendations on more appropriate thresholds that are also defensible.

The First Reaction

For the purpose of this article, let's take as our use case that an IRB (institutional review board) in an academic institution is requiring data to be de-identified according to the "0.04 percent standard." Oftentimes, when people hear a "0.04 percent" risk threshold requirement, they think a strict standard is being imposed, as the number "0.04 percent" sounds very small. This makes people wonder if imposing such a seemingly strict requirement constrains the sharing of health data for secondary purposes. Does this mean any data released will have limited utility? Is the IRB being perhaps overly conservative? Are we entering the era of over-restrictive data sharing?

In fact, it turns out the "0.04 percent" is paradoxical in that its logic represents an impossible standard to meet while the actual value represents quite a permissive standard—at least more permissive than other commonly used standards that have a much stronger precedent.

In order to fully grasp this issue, it is important to first understand re-identification risk measurement and the concept of "uniqueness."

"Uniqueness" as a Measure of Risk

The HIPAA Privacy Rule defines two standards for the de-identification of health information: Safe Harbor, and the Statistical Method (or the Expert Determination Method).

During consultations prior to the HIPAA Privacy Rule coming into effect and the publication of these standards, it was evident the Department of Health and Human Services (HHS) thought of "uniqueness" as the measure of re-identification risk (see the sidebar "Comments about Uniqueness by HHS").

Uniqueness here refers to uniqueness in the US population. For example, if "Sally" is the only ninety-year-old female in zip code 51210 based on census information, then Sally is unique. In a population data set, Sally's record will be the only one with these three values (age=ninety, gender=female, ZIP5=51210). The percentage of individuals in the population that are unique is referred to as "population uniqueness." For instance, when we say population uniqueness is 5 percent, this means 5 percent of the population in a particular geographic area has unique values on the variables we have selected. To be meaningful, one must specify the geography (for example, the whole of the United States, or just the state of California) and the fields that are used to compute uniqueness.

Not every data set will cover the whole population of the United States or a particular state. However, if the data set is a simple random sample from the population, then the percentage of records in the sample data set that are unique in the population will also be 5 percent. In our Sally example, if her record is in the sample data set, she will be unique

Comments about Uniqueness by HHS
In commentary about the Safe Harbor standard, the Federal Register notes[1,2] "the two main sources of disclosure risk for de-identified records about individuals are the existence of records with very unique characteristics (e.g., unusual occupation or very high salary or age) and the existence of external sources of records with matching data elements which can be used to link with the de-identified information and identify individuals (e.g., voter registration records or driver's license records). [. . .] an expert disclosure analysis would also consider the probability that an individual who is the target of an attempt at re-identification [sic] is represented on both files, the probability that the matching variables are recorded identically on the two types of records, the probability that the target individual is unique in the population for the matching variables, and the degree of confidence that a match would correctly identify a unique person."

in the sample. But she is also unique in the population. Therefore, Sally would be part of this 5 percent.

The Origins of the 0.04 Percent Threshold

> **Keypoints About Uniqueness:**
>
> - It is one measure of re-identification risk.
> - It is interpreted as the percentage of the population that is unique.
> - It can only be meaningfully interpreted if the set of variables and the geographic region are also specified.
> - The uniqueness of a simple random sample will be the same, on average, as the uniqueness in the population.

The Safe Harbor de-identification standard in the HIPAA Privacy Rule stipulates that sixteen data elements be removed from a data set, and two other data elements be generalized. The latter two elements are zip code (which should be generalized to the first three digits), and dates (which should be generalized to year). The Safe Harbor de-identification standard is summarized in Table 3.

The actual re-identification risk of Safe Harbor data sets has been computed empirically. One often cited analysis concluded that 0.04 percent of the US population is unique on their gender, age in years, and the first three digits of their zip code[3,4].

Using the 0.04 percent value as a basis for creating a de-identified data set is premised on the logic that this is the Safe Harbor risk value, and therefore it should be an acceptable basis for de-identifying any data set. If a Safe Harbor data set represents an acceptable risk level then it would represent an acceptable risk level for other data sets as well.

There are a number of fundamental problems with using this number as a risk threshold based on the logic above that are summarized below. These problems make it inadvisable to use that number as a threshold.

What's Wrong with the 0.04 Percent Threshold?

Poor Documentation and Inconsistent Definitions

Despite it being widely reported in various forms over the years, there is no clear documentation of the methodology that was used to derive the 0.04 percent number. As noted in the article by Luk Arbuckle ("The HIPAA Safe Harbor De-identification Standard and Uniqueness"), in addition to the 0.04 percent number, there are some articles saying the percentage of unique individuals in the US population on a Safe Harbor compliant data set is 0.00004 percent, some include month and year of birth (which is inconsistent with Safe Harbor), and some include the full non-extended five-digit zip (which is inconsistent with Safe Harbor). Therefore, it is not clear what the real number being claimed is, what fields it covers, and whether it really does characterize Safe Harbor risk.

The following identifiers of the individual, or of relatives, employers, or household members of the individual, are removed:

1. Names;
2. All geographic subdivisions smaller than a state, including street address, city, county, precinct, zip code, and their equivalent geo-codes, except for the initial three digits of a zip code if, according to the current publicly available data from the Bureau of the Census:
    a) The geographic unit formed by combining all zip codes with the same three initial digits contains more than twenty thousand people; and
    b) The initial three digits of a zip code for all such geographic units containing twenty thousand or fewer people is changed to 000.
3. All elements of dates (except year) for dates directly related to an individual, including birth date, admission date, discharge date, date of death; and all ages over eighty-nine and all elements of dates (including year) indicative of such age, except that such ages and elements may be aggregated into a single category of age ninety or older;
4. Telephone numbers;
5. Fax numbers;
6. Electronic mail addresses;
7. Social security numbers;
8. Medical record numbers;
9. Health plan beneficiary numbers;
10. Account numbers;
11. Certificate/license numbers;
12. Vehicle identifiers and serial numbers, including license plate numbers;
13. Device identifiers and serial numbers;
14. Web Universal Resource Locators (URLs);
15. Internet Protocol (IP) address numbers;
16. Biometric identifiers, including finger and voice prints;
17. Full face photographic images and any comparable images; and
18. Any other unique identifying number, characteristic, or code.

Table 1: The 18 elements to be removed or generalized for a Safe Harbor compliant data set.

Impossible Logic

The logic of using the 0.04 percent value is that the Safe Harbor risk is a good baseline to use. However, the Safe Harbor risk will change over time as the population changes (grows) over time.

With the publicly available 2000 US census data containing age, gender, and ZIP3 (first three digits) values, it is relatively easy to compute the population uniqueness values directly from that data, which we did. The results of our analysis of the 2000 census data found that the proportion of unique individuals on these three values is less than 0.0001 percent. Using the 2010 census data, the proportion of unique individuals in the US population on a Safe Harbor compliant data set is *zero*, which means there are no unique individuals anymore in the US for a Safe Harbor data set.

If we continue to apply the same logic for using the 0.04 percent threshold, we should now use zero as the threshold based on the latest available evidence. A zero threshold means no data can be de-identified. No useful data set that is released will meet this zero threshold. This demonstrates how the basic logic of using the 0.04 percent as a threshold is flawed.

Quite Conservative Risk Level

A Safe Harbor compliant data set can have a risk that is much higher than the 0.04 percent. For example, consider the data set below in Table 4. Here we have three records that are each unique on gender, age in years, and ZIP3. If an adversary knows the individuals in the data set then all of the records are unique. This means 100 percent of the records are unique instead of 0.04 percent. In this case, the 0.04 percent is much lower than the Safe Harbor risk.

Gender	Age	ZIP3	Clinical Information (e.g., diagnosis)
M	55	112	Diabetes
F	53	114	Stroke
M	24	134	Wrist Fracture

Table 2: A Safe Harbor Compliant Data Set

Quite Permissive Risk Level

In practice, a risk threshold has two components: the probability threshold itself; and the percentage of records that are allowed to be above the probability threshold. If one sets the second value (percentage of records above the probability threshold) to zero, then only the probability threshold value itself is used. But in the example we are examining here, there are two components that need to be considered.

To use the 0.04 percent threshold correctly, it must be clear that it refers to the fact that no more than 0.04 percent of the records in a data set are *unique*.

Using uniqueness as the basis for our probability threshold means we will allow records in the data set that have a probability of re-identification of 0.5. Yes, that is correct—we would allow records in the data set where the chance of re-identification is at half, a one in two chance. The Safe Harbor-derived threshold described above allows up to 99.96 percent of the records to have a probability of re-identification that is as high as 0.5. Most observers would say this is a high-probability threshold. If I had a voter registration list and tried to match it with such a data set, the expected proportion of records that would be matched correctly would be as high as 50 percent.

Allowing such a high-probability threshold is quite permissive by most standards.

When we were contemplating this issue, we developed an IRB Wizard tool based on the year 2000 US census data that can be used to automate these calculations. This tool, which is available on our website, is intended to illustrate risk variations across the country and allows you to assess whether the re-identification risk is below this threshold for various regions in the United States for basic demographics. Let us consider a few examples.

Figure 1 shows that 0.019 percent of the population of California is unique on ZIP5 (full non-extended zip) and the year of birth. This is more detail than is allowed by Safe Harbor but is still below 0.04 percent. In figure 2 we see that ZIP3 (first three digits), gender, and the month and year of birth also represent lower uniqueness than the threshold.

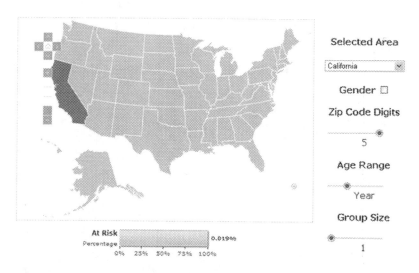

Figure 1: Population uniqueness with ZIP5, and year of birth for the state of California

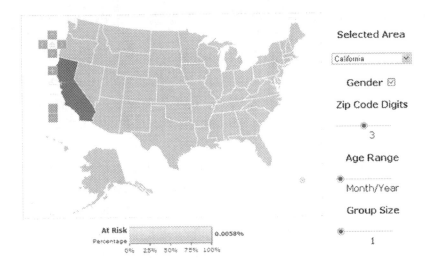

Figure 2: Population uniqueness with gender, ZIP3, and month/year of birth for the state of California

A more commonly used probability threshold is 0.2 (equivalent to a "cell size of 5"). If we use that probability threshold on the same scenarios that we examined above, we would find that the percentage of the population that is high risk is higher compared to uniqueness (see Figure 3 and Figure 4). For example, Zip5 and age in years for California has 0.17 percent above the 0.2 probability threshold, but only 0.019 percent above the 0.5 (uniqueness) probability threshold. This is not surprising because the uniqueness threshold is quite permissive.

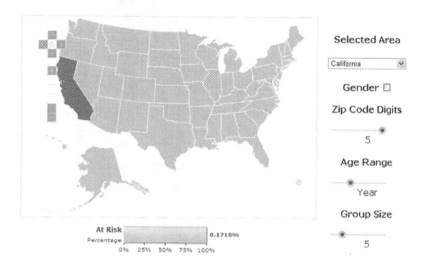

Figure 3: Population in groups of size 5 or less with ZIP5 and year of birth for the state of California

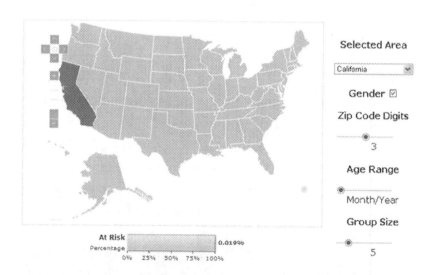

Figure 4: Population in groups of size 5 or less with gender, ZIP3, and month/year of birth for the state of California

The disclosure control community considers any grouping level below 3 to be inappropriately small[5]. This means that in general uniqueness is not considered a good standard to use because the risk threshold of 0.5 is simply too high.

Context Independent

The concept of using the same risk threshold for all data disclosures presents a problem. Consider the two extremes: (a) releasing data to a trusted researcher or business partner; and (b) the public disclosure of data on the web. Using a single threshold that is suitable for scenario (a) means the risk is too high for scenario (b). Using a single threshold that is suitable for scenario (b) means the risk is too low (conservative) for scenario (a). Because a single risk value is context independent, it will be either too high or too low for some portion of data disclosures.

Poor Precedent

As the analysis in the article by Luk Arbuckle referenced above shows, an alternative way to measure Safe Harbor risk is to evaluate the average probability rather than look at uniqueness. The table in that article shows a national average probability of re-identification around 0.05 percent, and the variations by state, for a Safe Harbor data set. However, there are other probability thresholds that have a much stronger precedent for the disclosure of sensitive information, such as the "cell size of 5" rule. These precedents have been in use for decades and have provided, when used, adequate protection. In fact, there is also very little precedent for the 0.05 percent number.

Final Recommendations

It is not recommended to use the 0.04 percent threshold in practice. It is a flawed number based on a flawed logic and has weak precedents, and the probability threshold is not recommended by the disclosure control community. There are other ways to build on Safe Harbor to choose a probability threshold or use thresholds that have a much stronger precedent and justification. In other articles we discuss these alternatives.

References

1. Department of Health and Human Services, *"Standards for Privacy of Individually Identifiable Health Information,"* http://aspe.hhs.gov/admnsimp/final/PvcFR06.txt, Federal Register, 2000.
2. Department of Health and Human Services, *"Standards for Privacy of Individually Identifiable Health Information,"* http://aspe.hhs.gov/admnsimp/final/PvcFR05.txt, Federal Register, 2000.
3. National Committee on Vital and Health Statistics, *"Report to the Secretary of the US Department of Health and Human Services on Enhanced Protections for Uses of Health Data: A Stewardship Framework for 'Secondary Uses' of Electronically Collected and Transmitted Health Data,"* 2007.
4. Latanya Sweeney, *"Data Sharing under HIPAA: Twelve Years Later"* (Workshop on the HIPAA Privacy Rule's De-identification Standard), http://www.hhshipaaprivacy.com, 2010.
5. Leon Willenborg, and Ton de Waal, *Statistical Disclosure Control in Practice*, New York: Springer-Verlag, 1996.

THE HIPAA SAFE HARBOR DE-IDENTIFICATION STANDARD AND UNIQUENESS

Luk Arbuckle

Previous and much quoted studies by Sweeney[1,2] have claimed that applying Safe Harbor standards[3] to US census data result in a data set with 0.04 percent of the population being unique. This number has also been quoted in a report to the secretary of the US Department of Health and Human Services (HHS)[4]. The original work[5,6] that came up with this estimate is based on census data from 1990 and makes no mention of Safe Harbor. In fact, the number 0.04 percent [5,6]refers to uniqueness based on the quasi-identifiers of month and year of birth, gender, and county (referred to as Safe Harbor[1]), or year of birth, gender, and five-digit zip code. However, neither of these sets of quasi-identifiers are compliant with Safe Harbor standards[3].

According to 45 CFR 164.514 (2)(i)(B), compliant health data may contain three-digit zip codes if there are more than twenty thousand people in the resulting geographic unit, and the zip code 000 otherwise. Further, according to 45 CFR 164.514 (2)(i)(C), only dates in years may be provided, including ages up to eighty-nine and top-coded as ninety-plus[3]. Referring to Sweeney's work[5,6], the set of variables that best reflect the Safe Harbor standards would therefore be year of birth, gender, and county, and as shown in these references, this results in 0.00004 percent of the population being unique. The often quoted 0.04 percent is therefore a thousand times greater than this result. Given the discrepancies found in the literature, and to update the estimate of the population that is unique under Safe Harbor standards[3], we repeated the calculations of uniqueness based on US census data from 2010, and found no unique individuals. This is similar to the estimates of nearly zero based on 1990 census data in[5,6], and 2000 census data in[7]. If we were to define a Safe Harbor risk threshold standard on US census data today, we would therefore not allow there to be any unique individuals in data sets.

To estimate uniqueness in the entire US population, we considered the quasi-identifiers of year of birth, gender, and three-digit zip code for populations over twenty thousand, and the zip code 000 otherwise; to estimate uniqueness by US states, we considered the quasi-identifiers year of birth, gender, state, and three-digit zip code for populations over twenty thousand, and the zip code 000 otherwise. The distinction when evaluating uniqueness by state is that some three-digit zip codes cross state boundaries and must therefore be considered separately to ensure the populations are over twenty thousand (otherwise they are added to the zip code 000).

Although none of the population was found to be unique in the US census data from 2010 under Safe Harbor standards[3], this is not to say there is no risk of re-identification. We consider the risk exposure for different groups based on the number of records in a set of quasi-identifiers (i.e., year of birth, gender, three-digit zip code). In general, risk exposure is defined as the cost of an event (loss) times the probability of the event that induces the loss. In our context the loss is the number of people that are at risk of re-identification, and the probability is therefore the probability of re-identification. A set of quasi-identifiers is called an equivalence class, and the size of the equivalence class is the number of people in the equivalence class. We consider the risk exposure re_i for all records in equivalence classes of size i, given by loss l_i with probability P_i. That is:

$$re_i = l_i \times P_i = \left(N \times p_i\right) \times \left(\frac{1}{i}\right) = \frac{N_i}{i} = J_i,$$

where N is the population size, p_i is the proportion of records in equivalence classes of size i, N_i is the number of people in equivalence classes of size i, and J_i is the expected number of people in equivalence classes of size i that are at risk of re-identification.

With this in mind, we plotted the results of the risk exposure for different equivalence class sizes in Figure 1. Recall that these results are based on US census data from 2010 and Safe Harbor standards[3]. The plot shows how many people are at risk of re-identification based on year of birth, gender, and three-digit zip code for a large number of equivalence class sizes.

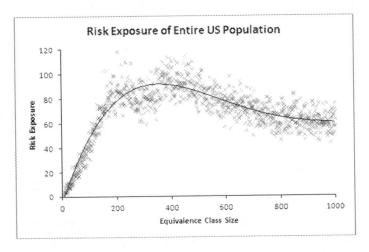

Figure 1—Risk exposure for entire US population in 2010, following Safe Harbor standards.[3]

In Figure 1 we consider the total risk exposure across all equivalence class sizes, also called a "marketer risk" in the Privacy Analytics Risk Assessment Tool (PARAT) for each state. This is equivalent to the area under the risk exposure curve. Again we see how few people are at risk, based on US census data from 2010 and Safe Harbor standards[3]. For the entire US population in 2010, only 0.051 percent is at risk of re-identification. This number is close to the commonly used 0.04 percent threshold, but its meaning and empirical basis are very different and should not be confused with one another, despite how close they are numerically.

State	Mean Population at Risk	Population	Risk Exposure (percent)
AK	900	709,930	0.127 percent
AL	3,240	4,779,718	0.068 percent
AR	2,520	2,915,912	0.086 percent
AZ	2,160	6,391,933	0.034 percent
CA	10,260	37,249,968	0.028 percent
CO	3,060	5,029,196	0.061 percent
CT	1,800	3,574,097	0.050 percent
DC	180	601,723	0.030 percent
DE	540	897,934	0.060 percent
FL	4,500	18,801,226	0.024 percent
GA	3,600	9,687,632	0.037 percent
HI	360	1,360,301	0.026 percent
IA	4,500	3,046,355	0.148 percent
ID	1,260	1,567,573	0.080 percent
IL	5,220	12,830,628	0.041 percent
IN	3,600	6,483,802	0.056 percent
KS	3,420	2,853,116	0.120 percent
KY	4,860	4,339,367	0.112 percent
LA	2,340	4,533,310	0.052 percent
MA	3,240	6,547,626	0.049 percent
MD	2,340	5,773,552	0.041 percent
ME	1,980	1,328,358	0.149 percent
MI	3,600	9,883,638	0.036 percent

MN	2,700	5,303,924	0.051 percent
MO	4,500	5,988,927	0.075 percent
MS	2,160	2,967,297	0.073 percent
MT	1,800	989,399	0.182 percent
NC	3,600	9,535,477	0.038 percent
ND	1,620	672,591	0.241 percent
NE	2,160	1,826,341	0.118 percent
NH	1,440	1,316,470	0.109 percent
NJ	3,600	8,791,894	0.041 percent
NM	1,980	2,058,679	0.096 percent
NV	1,080	2,700,536	0.040 percent
NY	8,820	19,378,077	0.046 percent
OH	5,220	11,536,504	0.045 percent
OK	3,060	3,751,345	0.082 percent
OR	1,800	3,831,067	0.047 percent
PA	8,280	12,702,375	0.065 percent
PR	540	3,723,066	0.015 percent
RI	360	1,052,567	0.034 percent
SC	1,800	4,625,364	0.039 percent
SD	1,440	814,180	0.177 percent
TN	2,700	6,346,105	0.043 percent
TX	8,460	25,145,164	0.034 percent
UT	1,260	2,763,855	0.046 percent
VA	5,040	8,001,019	0.063 percent
VT	1,440	625,741	0.230 percent
WA	2,520	6,724,540	0.037 percent
WI	3,240	5,686,986	0.057 percent
WV	3,960	1,852,994	0.214 percent
WY	1,800	563,618	0.319 percent
US	158,580	312,462,997	0.051 percent

Figure 1: Total risk exposure by state population in 2010, following Safe Harbor standards[3]

If the metric used to de-identify data were equivalent to applying Safe Harbor standards to US census data, then no unique individuals would be allowed. But this is a very narrow view and ignores all other equivalence classes. Rather, a more appropriate metric would be risk exposure. As has been shown here, this metric still results in a very strict standard. Applied to other data sets, it would require an adversary know every quasi-identifier exactly, which may be too strong an assumption. However, the point is that if you are going to use Safe Harbor standards and US census data to define a metric, careful application and interpretation are imperative.

References

1. Latanya Sweeney, *"Data Sharing under HIPAA: Twelve Years Later,"* Washington, DC, March 8, 2010.
2. Latanya Sweeney, *"Patient Identifiability in Pharmaceutical Marketing Data,"* Harvard University, Cambridge, MA, WP-1015, January 2011.
3. Department of Health and Human Services, *"Administrative Data Standards and Related Requirements, Public Welfare, Code of Federal Regulations,"* Federal Register 45, no. Parts 160, 162, and 164 (October 2007): 696-785.
4. National Committee on Vital and Health Statistics, *"Enhanced Protections for Uses of Health Data: A Stewardship Framework for 'Secondary Uses' of Electronically Collected and Transmitted Health Data,"* Washington, DC, Report to the Secretary of the US Department of Health and Human Services, December 2007.
5. Latanya Sweeney, *"Uniqueness of Simple Demographics in the US Population,"* Carnegie Mellon University, Pittsburgh, PA, WP-4, 2000.
6. Latanya Sweeney, *"Simple Demographics Often Identify People Uniquely,"* Carnegie Mellon University, Pittsburgh, PA, WP-3, 2000.
7. Philippe Golle, *"Revisiting the Uniqueness of Simple Demographics in the US Population,"* Proceedings of the 5th ACM Workshop on Privacy in Electronic Society, New York, NY, 2006, 77-80.

ON THE LIMITS OF THE SAFE HARBOR DE-IDENTIFICATION STANDARD

Khaled El Emam

The HIPAA Privacy Rule defines two standards for the de-identification of health data. The first standard is Safe Harbor. The Safe Harbor standard specifies eighteen data elements that must be removed or generalized in a data set. A listing of these eighteen data elements can be found in the previous article, "De-identification and Masking: The Differences and Why It Is Optimal to Utilize Both Techniques to Protect Data". If that is done, the data set is considered de-identified. Because of its simplicity, Safe Harbor is popular. Implementing Safe Harbor does not require technical knowledge about de-identification or re-identification risk. It also provides certainty—if you make this set of well-defined changes, you would be meeting the standard.

However, Safe Harbor also has an important disadvantage: it does not actually ensure the risk of re-identification is low except in very limited circumstances. I would also argue that these circumstances are quite rare in practice. Let me explain.

Let us consider the situation where a data custodian is disclosing data publicly (say on the web). In this case, the data custodian is creating a public-use file (without any terms of use). I am choosing this scenario because when doing a risk assessment, one should consider the probability of an adversary attempting to re-identify a record. Under these conditions we do not have to worry about analyzing the probability of an attempted re-identification because with a public-use file, we assume this probability is always one, which in statistical terms, means it is certain. Therefore, when creating a public file we have to assume someone will attempt to re-identify the data because there are no controls that can realistically be put in place to prohibit that.

Going back to our example, let's say the data custodian has applied the Safe Harbor standard to the public-use file. Below are situations where the public-use file will have a high risk of re-identification even though it meets that standard.

The Adversary Knows Who Is in the Data

Consider the simple data set below (Table 1), which has been disclosed. This data set meets the Safe Harbor conditions in that the age is in years, and only the first three digits of the zip code are given. If the adversary knows "Tom" is in this data set, and that Tom is fifty-five, the adversary will know with absolute certainty that the first record belongs to Tom. Here we have the highest risk of re-identification possible for this record. In fact, because all the ages are unique, just knowing the age of an individual who is in the data set will result in re-identification with certainty.

A logical question related to this scenario is: How can an adversary know Tom is in the data set? There are a number of ways, as exemplified below. First, the data set can be a population registry, so everyone with a particular disease, for instance, will be in the data set. For example, if this is a diabetes registry, and if

119

Tom has diabetes, he will be in the data set. Second, if the data set is from a study, Tom may self-reveal by posting the information on his Facebook page, for example, that he participated in said study and is therefore in the data set. Third, if consent to participate was required from a substitute decision maker or a parent, then that consenting individual will know Tom is in the data set. Finally, if the data set is from a study of employees who volunteered, and coworkers know who took the day off to participate in the study, then the coworkers would know Tom was in the data set. Therefore, inclusion may be "knowable."

One way to address this concern is to only disclose a simple random sample rather than a complete data set. This adds uncertainty as to whether Tom is in the data set or not. Of course, one has to be careful in choosing the sampling fraction, or what percentage of records to release, to ensure that this uncertainty is large enough, and that requires some analytical thought.

Gender	Age	ZIP3	Lab Test
M	55	112	Albumin, Serum
F	53	114	Creatine Kinase
M	54	134	Alkaline Phosphatase

Table 1: Safe Harbor compliant data set

The Data Set is Not a Random Sample from the US Population

During the analysis that led to the Safe Harbor standard, the re-identification risk of data sets that meet the standard was deemed low if the data set was a simple random sample from the US population. However, if the data set is not a simple random sample then the risk can still be very high. Let me explain through an example of a simulation described below.

I took the hospital discharge database for the state of New York for 2007. After cleaning, removing incomplete, redundant, or duplicated information, etc., this database consists of approximately 1.5 million individuals who have been hospitalized. I then took 50% random samples of patients from that data set and evaluated how many individual patients were unique in the sample and also unique in the population. This sampling process was repeated 1000 times and the uniqueness averaged across the iterations. Any sample meets two criteria: (a) hospitalized individuals in New York are not a simple random sample from the US population, and (b) an adversary who knows that Tom has been hospitalized would not know if he is in the selected sample or not.

If I take a cohort of males over 65 years who have been hospitalized for more than 14 days, and know only their age in years, gender, and 3 digit ZIP code from the sample data set, this group had a uniqueness of 4%, and those hospitalized more than 30 days had a uniqueness of 11.14%. Therefore, by restricting or refining the cohort further and further, the individuals in the sample become more and more unique in the population of hospitalized patients in New York.

High uniqueness is bad because it means that if I find a match to Tom, it is a correct match with certainty. Even if I do not know if Tom is in the data set, if I find a record that matches him in the disclosed Safe Harbor data set then I will know that it is Tom's record.

Other Fields Can be Used for Re-identification

It is common for health data sets to have other kinds of fields that can be used for re-identification beyond the set included in Safe Harbor. Here we consider some examples of data elements that would pass the Safe Harbor standard but would still produce a data set with a high probability of re-identification.

An example of a data set that is fairly easy to re-identify is a longitudinal data set. Longitudinal data contains information about multiple visits or episodes of care. For example, let us consider the state inpatient database for New York for the year 2007 again, which contains information on just over 2 million visits. Some patients had multiple visits and their ZIP code changed from one visit to the next. If we consider that the age and gender are fixed, and allow the three digit ZIP code to change across visits (and the adversary knows those zip codes), then 1.8 percent of the patients are unique. If we assume the adversary also knows the length of stay for each of the visits, then 20.75 percent of the patients are unique. Note that length of stay is not covered by Safe Harbor and therefore can be included in the data set. Longitudinal information such as the patient's three-digit zip code and length of stay may be known by neighbors, coworkers, relatives, and ex-spouses, as well as in the public eye for famous people. As can be seen, there is a significant increase in uniqueness when the three-digit zip code is treated longitudinally, and a dramatic increase when other visit information is added to the data set.

Although fields such as diagnosis and procedure codes are important for many analytics on health data, the reality is, this is the kind of information an adversary would know. An adversary may not know the precise diagnosis code (i.e., ICD-9 code) of a patient but may know the general diagnosis (e.g., the site of a cancer or that it was a heart attack). Therefore, it behooves the data custodian to consider this additional information when examining re-identification risk. Put another way, it would be difficult to justify not including this kind of information in a re-identification risk assessment. In longitudinal data sets there are many diagnoses and procedures that increase the risk of re-identification.

By specifying a precise and limited set of fields to consider, the Safe Harbor standard provides a simple "cookie cutter" approach to de-identification. However, it also ignores the many other data fields that can be used to re-identify individuals, reducing its effectiveness at providing meaningful universal protections for different kinds of data sets.

Conclusions

Unless the data set being disclosed only has the fields specified in Safe Harbor, is a simple cross-sectional data set, or is a simple random sample, data custodians need to be careful about relying on the Safe Harbor standard as the basis for de-identification. It would be challenging to demonstrate that using the Safe Harbor standard ensures a low re-identification risk on many real-world data sets unless they are the most basic type of data sets.

A prudent approach, from a risk management perspective, is to follow the second HIPAA de-identification standard instead, which relies on the statistical method. This second standard can take into account the subtleties of such data sets that Safe Harbor fails to address, thus allowing data custodians to still release data but have peace of mind that they are at a low risk of re-identification.

DE-IDENTIFICATION AND MASKING: THE DIFFERENCES AND WHY IT IS OPTIMAL TO UTILIZE BOTH TECHNIQUES TO PROTECT DATA

Khaled El Emam

There has been some confusion in the health data community about the difference between "masking" and "de-identification." This may partially be due to the proliferation of different terms describing the same thing, and the same terms describing different things; for example, one sees terms such "obfuscation," "anonymization," and "coding." In this article, I will clarify the distinction between masking and de-identification.

We need to start with a few definitions. In a data set we make a distinction between two types of variables: direct identifiers and quasi-identifiers (also known as indirect identifiers). Direct identifiers are fields that can uniquely identify individuals, such as names, social security numbers, and e-mail addresses. Direct identifiers are often not used in any statistical analyses that are run on the health data. Quasi-identifiers are fields that can identify individuals but are also useful for data analysis. Examples of these include dates, demographic information (such as race and ethnicity), and socioeconomic variables. This distinction is important because the techniques used to protect the variables will depend on how they are classified.

Masking refers to a set of techniques that attempt to protect direct identifiers. There are a set of common and defensible approaches for masking direct identifiers:

1. **Variable Suppression**

   This involves the removal of the direct identifiers from the data set. Suppression is used more in data uses and disclosures for research and public health purposes. In those contexts it is not necessary to have the identifying variables in the data set.

2. **Randomization**

   Randomization keeps all the direct identifiers in the data set but replaces their values with fake (random) values. If done properly, the probability of reverse engineering the masked values would be very small. The most common use-case for randomization is creating data sets for software testing. This means data is pulled from production databases, masked, and then sent to the development team for testing. Because testing expects data according to a fixed data schema, it is necessary to retain all the fields and have realistic-looking values in there.

3. **Shuffling**

   These methods take one value from a record and switch it with a value from another record. In this case, all the values in the data set are real, but they are assigned to the wrong people.

4. **Creating Pseudonyms**

   The creation of pseudonyms can be done in one of two ways. Both should be performed on unique patient values (e.g., SSNs or medical record numbers). One approach is to apply a one-way hash to the value using a secret key (this key must be protected). A hash is a function that converts a value to another value (the hash value), but you cannot reverse the hash value back to the original value. This approach has the advantage that it can be recreated accurately at a later point on a different data set. The second approach is to create a random pseudonym that cannot be recreated. Each has utility for different use cases.

Some companies employ techniques in masking tools that do not provide meaningful protection, including the following:

1. **Adding Noise**

   The challenge with noise addition (which is most relevant for continuous variables) is problematic because there are many techniques that have been developed to remove noise out of data. Therefore, a sophisticated adversary can remove the noise from the data using various filters and recover the original values. There are many types of filters that have been developed in the signal-processing domain.

2. **Character Scrambling**

   Some masking tools will rearrange the order of the characters in a field. For example, "SMITH" may be scrambled to "TMHIS." This is quite easy to reverse. To illustrate, I took the surname table published by the US Census Bureau from the 2000 census. It has 151,671 unique surnames. Out of the names there were 113,242 combinations of characters. There were 91,438 unique combinations of characters (i.e., they are the only name with that combination of characters). That means that just by knowing the characters in a name, I can figure out the name 60 percent of the time because the characters that make up that name are unique. Another 13,721 have combinations of characters that appear in two names. As you can see, this is not a reliable way to protect information.

3. **Character Masking**

   Character masking is when the last one or more characters of a string are replaced with an asterisk ("*"). An important decision is how many characters should be replaced in such a manner. In the surname example, we replaced the last character with a "*." In total, there were 102,312 (approximately 67 percent) of the names that still had a unique combination of characters. If two characters are replaced, 69,300 names are still unique (~46 percent). Without metrics to assess how many characters to replace, this type of masking may be giving a false sense of security when in fact the ability to accurately guess the name may be quite high.

4. **Truncation**

   Truncation is a variant of character masking in that the last few characters are removed rather than replaced with a "*." This can also have the same risks as character masking. For example, the removal of the last character in a name still results in approximately 67 percent of the names being unique on the remaining characters.

5. **Encoding**

   Encoding is when the value is replaced with another meaningless value. This process must be done with care because it is easy to perform a frequency analysis and figure out the names by how often they appear. For example, in a multiracial data set, the most frequent name is likely to be "SMITH." Encoding should be performed only in the context of creating pseudonyms on unique values and not as a general masking function. The masking techniques that are not protective should not be used in practice. A data custodian is taking a nontrivial risk otherwise.

It is important to keep in mind that even the masking techniques that are protective will significantly reduce the utility of the data. Therefore, masking should only be applied to the fields that will not be used in any data analysis, which are often the direct identifiers—fields such as names and e-mail addresses that are not usually part of any analysis performed on the data. Also, one should not apply masking techniques to dates or geographic information because these fields are often used in data analysis, and masking would make it difficult to perform an analysis using those fields.

6. **De-identification** is based on characteristics of the different variables and field type. For instance, different algorithms are applied to dates of birth than are applied to Zip codes.[1] Many data sets consist of both quasi-identifiers and direct identifiers. In practice it is important to apply both data protection techniques: masking and de-identification.

References

1. Khaled El Emam, FidaKamal Dankar, Romeo Issa, Elizabeth Jonker, Daniel Amyot, Elise Cogo, Jean-Pierre Corriveau, Mark Walker, Sadrul Chowdhury, Regis Vaillancourt, Tyson Roffey, Jim Bottomley, "A Global k-Anonymity Method for the De-Identification of Health Data", http://171.67.114.118/content/16/5/670. full, JAMIA, June 2, 2009

THE FALSE PROMISE OF DATA MASKING

Khaled El Emam

Let me start with some good news. Increasingly, I am encountering IT departments that are recognizing that they need to protect the privacy of data subjects in their databases when they use and disclose those databases for secondary purposes. Secondary purposes can be, for instance, IT sending their patient data to an outside consulting company to use for testing their business software applications. Oftentimes, IT departments will also be consulted by business lines when they have new initiatives that require the disclosure of data to external parties. It is at this time that IT should bring up the privacy issue.

However, many are still only resorting to simplistic masking techniques to achieve this privacy protection. As I described in a previous article (see De-identification and Masking: The Differences and Why it is Optimal to Utilize Both Techniques to Protect Data), relying only on masking has a number of distinct disadvantages.

Masking Effectively Eliminates Analytic Utility in Data

First of all, many of the masking techniques that are commonly used will destroy the data utility in the masked fields. This means that any relationships among masked variables or between masked and non-masked variables are removed. With some masking techniques, such as shuffling, it is possible to have accurate summary statistics about a single field at a time; but not when you want to look at relationships. For most data analytics purposes this is quite limiting.

To illustrate this, I created two fields that had a correlation of 0.8 between them. After I shuffled the two fields using the most common approach—independent shuffling, the correlation sank to zero. When I shuffled only one of them it was 0.05. Therefore, standard shuffling is not recommended if the analytics that will be performed on the data involve the investigation of relationships. But most data analysis involves the investigation of relationships.

Masking Does Not Necessarily Protect Against Identity Disclosure

Secondly, data masking methods are not necessarily protective of privacy. Protecting against identity disclosure is a legal or regulatory requirement. This means that to ensure a data set does not contain personal information when disclosed for secondary purposes without patient consent or authorization, legal or regulatory compliance is required. For example, the HIPAA Privacy Rule states "Health information that does not identify an individual and with respect to which there is no reasonable basis to believe that the information can be used to identify an individual is not individually identifiable health information" [CFR 164.514(a)]. There exist certain expectations about how to do that. An IT department may be putting the organization at a legal or significant compliance risk position by using certain masking techniques. One cannot just make stuff up, label it as masking, and then magically it becomes acceptable to use. Let me illustrate such risks with a real example.

An organization has replaced patient identifying information in a database by creating pseudonyms, which is a data masking technique. Unfortunately a data breach occurred and that database was lost. During the subsequent investigation the regulator working on the file concluded that despite the fact that pseudonyms were utilized, there were other demographics and diagnosis fields in the database that rendered the masking useless and showed the data to still be personal health information. This is because the risk of re-identification of the patients is quite high. Now the organization will incur the breach notification costs.

Masking did not save the day.

But why did this happen? The data was masked wasn't it? In another article (see De-identification and Masking: The Differences and Why it is Optimal to Utilize Both Techniques to Protect Data) I provided some examples as to why simple masking techniques do not protect against the re-identification of patients. Let me dig deeper into this issue.

Masking techniques do not use metrics to measure what the actual risk of re-identification is, and therefore it is not always possible to know whether the transformations performed on the data were sufficient and were defensible. Not using metrics can be acceptable if the masking method itself is guaranteed to ensure a low probability of re-identification. I will give you an example where it is possible to ensure that the risk of re-identification was low without explicit metrics, and one where this is not the case.

In some instances we know that the probability of re-identification is going to be very small. For example, if we do random first name replacement and the database that we select from is large (say 10000 names) and the replacement names are chosen using a uniform distribution, then the probability of guessing any of the names in the database is 1/10000. This is a very small probability and the risk of reverse engineering the randomized names will be negligible. The same can be said for techniques such as the replacement facility names and replacement addresses. Therefore, randomization is a safe data masking technique.

However, there will also be situations where data masking can result in data releases where the risk is high. To illustrate this, I used a common masking technique to crop the last one or two digits of the ZIP code. Without measuring the re-identification risk it is not possible to know whether this was protective enough or not. Let's consider an example. I used the discharge abstract data set for the state of New York and a risk threshold of 0.2 (i.e. a probability equal to or less than 0.2 is acceptable). When we consider the month and year of birth, gender, and ZIP5 for all patient visits, 57.3% of the records have a probability of re-identification higher than 0.2. Cropping only one digit and retaining four digits of the ZIP code would mean that 25.3% of the records are high risk. If I cropped the ZIP code to only the first three digits, 5.5% of my records still have a re-identification risk that is higher than my threshold. By cropping without measuring the risk the data custodian would not know that more than 5% of their records have a high risk of re-identification. Methods like cropping (which may also be called truncation) should not be used as a form of masking because you cannot know whether the data has been protected enough. Without metrics, an analyst may over- or under-truncate. The problem is that the organization may find this out at the worst possible time—when a breach has occurred.

Things to Keep in Mind

To have defensible compliance with regulations and avoid costly breaches, the general rules are:

- Only mask fields that you will not perform any analytics on.
- Since masking is not based on risk measurement, only use masking methods that can guarantee a low risk, such as random value replacement from a large database.
- For all other fields use metric-based data transformations so you can know when you have reached acceptable levels of risk that is achieved by using standard de-identification techniques.
- Both masking and measurement-based de-identification are necessary to cover all of the fields in a typical health data set.

Otherwise the organization may be taking expensive chances with vanilla masking methods.

There are many data masking techniques available today, with a key differentiator being whether they can mask static databases or can mask "on-the-fly". In fact, neither of these criteria matter because unless the transformations done on the data, statically or dynamically, actually provide meaningful privacy protections, where and how fast you mask will not help protect the organizations from risks.

THE TWELVE CHARACTERISTICS OF A DE-IDENTIFICATION METHODOLOGY

Khaled El Emam

How can you know if a particular de-identification methodology is acceptable? Will its application produce results that would be acceptable to regulators? These questions are becoming increasingly relevant today for a number of reasons: (a) organizations are developing their own de-identification methodologies in-house and they need some way to assess them, (b) a number of masking and de-identification tool vendors have developed methodologies that they have been using in practice with their clients, and (c) de-identification consultants are also using methodologies for the de-identification and certification of health data.

Fortunately there are a series of guidance documents, codes of practice, and best practice guidelines available. We shall collectively refer to these as "standards". The "Relevant Reading" section at the end of this article lists some key standards. These documents provide us a basis to extract twelve key criteria that can be considered important for a de-identification methodology to meet.

The Requirements for a De-identification Methodology

1. Is the methodology documented?

Documenting the methodology is a critical step to ensure that it is repeatable and replicable. The documentation needs to list the steps required to evaluate re-identification risk and also to perform the actual de-identification. It is unlikely that all subjectivity in the process can be removed completely; but to the extent possible, there should be sufficient detail to achieve consistency between different experts performing de-identification.

It should be noted that a methodology is not just a set of technical approaches to de-identify a data set. There are many academic papers and text books giving chapter after chapter of specific techniques. A methodology would not just provide these techniques, but also produce a rationale for their application.

The steps in a methodology do not have to be all manual. Some steps can be supported through automation. But the methodology needs to explain what the steps being automated are.

2. Has the methodology received external or independent scrutiny?

There are number of methodologies that are currently in use to de-identify health data. Some are proprietary and some are available publicly. Regulators have emphasized the importance of transparency when de-identifying data sets. This means making the details of the methodology generally available.

There are a number of advantages to this kind of transparency. The first is ensuring to the data subjects (e.g., the patients whose data is being disclosed) that there is a documented methodology being used to de-identify their data. Unless the methodology is remarkably weak, this will help maintain public and patient trust.

Additionally, this public methodology must be open for scrutiny from other disclosure control experts and regulators. This ensures that weaknesses in the methodology are detected in a timely manner, and the regulators have an understanding of the methods being used in practice.

3. Does the methodology require and have a process for the explicit identification of the data custodian and the data recipients?

It seems somewhat obvious that one needs to identify the data custodian and the data recipient. There may be multiple data custodians and multiple data recipients. Each of these data recipients may have a different risk profile, resulting in multiple de-identification efforts. A methodology needs to include a step or steps for understanding the data flows for the particular use or disclosure, and subsequently identify all of the data custodians and data recipients for each use.

For example, a data set may have internal users and may also be disclosed externally to a business partner. Normally these would be treated as two different de-identification efforts because the contexts are different. If a single de-identified data set is created this might be too stringent or too permissive for one of the data recipients. In this case determining that there were two data recipients is therefore more than an academic or simple documentation exercise.

4. Does the methodology require and have a process for the identification of plausible adversaries and plausible attacks on the data?

To ensure that the appropriate amount of de-identification is performed, it is important to understand who the plausible

136

adversaries are and how they might try to re-identify the data. For example, if a data set is disclosed to a business partner then one can treat that business partner at two levels. The first level is the business partner itself being a potential adversary. At the second level there may be a rogue employee at the business partner as a legal entity who may be an adversary. The threats from each of these two scenarios are quite different, and the management of re-identification risk under these two scenarios is also quite different. If a methodology does not provide templates or have a process for making these distinctions then important threats may not be considered during the de-identification exercise.

It is not sufficient to just say that the person creating a de-identification methodology has to identify adversaries and attacks. Guidance and steps ought to be provided to ensure a comprehensive and repeatable outcome.

5. Does the methodology require and have a process for the determination of direct identifiers and quasi-identifiers?

Data transformations will depend on whether a field in a data set is considered a direct identifier or a quasi-identifier. Documenting methods and criteria for the classification of fields accordingly is important. Normally this process involves examining the fields in a data set, their data types, relationships among the fields, and understanding their functions.

Sometimes a field may not be classified as an identifier or a quasi-identifier. For example, in an insurance data set there may be fields pertaining to the date a payer reimburses a provider. In many situations that date would not be considered a quasi-identifier because plausible adversaries would either not have that kind of information to launch or attack, or will already know the identity of the data subjects.

It is important that these decisions are explicitly documented because they may need to be justified in the case of an audit or an investigation.

6. Does the methodology have a process for identifying mitigating controls to manage any residual risks?

The current de-identification standards make clear that taking context into account is an important part of evaluating the risk of re-identification. In this case, context includes the practices of the data recipient, and whether there is a data use agreement in place with the data recipient. Such factors are called mitigating controls. Without the explicit consideration of mitigating controls too much, or too little, de-identification may be applied to a data set.

The methodology needs to identify the appropriate mitigating controls to consider (with justifications of course), how to evaluate their level of existence and implementation by the data recipient, and how to incorporate that evaluation in the overall process of de-identification. The steps need to be precise enough to allow the process to be repeatable.

7. Does the methodology require the measurement of actual re-identification risks for different types of attacks?

The measurement of re-identification risk is absolutely critical in any defensible de-identification methodology. Such measurements will provide the objective means to demonstrate that a particular data set has a very small risk of re-identification. Without empirical data, it is not possible to have a defensible case in the event of an audit or an investigation.

In order to measure the risk of re-identification, measurement instruments are needed. These instruments are the metrics which must be defined. The metrics chosen must be consistent with the plausible attacks that have been identified and the nature of the data (e.g., measuring risk for a population registry would be different from the measurement of risk for a sample).

8. Is it possible to set, in a defensible way, re-identification risk thresholds?

Identifiability falls on a continuous spectrum. However, regulations and privacy laws make a binary distinction between personal and non-personal information. The continuous spectrum of identifiability can be converted to this binary representation by defining a risk threshold. If the measured risk in the data is higher than the threshold then the data is considered to be personal information. If the measured risk is below the threshold then the data is considered not to be personal information. Therefore, the definition of thresholds is critical.

Existing de-identification standards make clear that such thresholds must be context dependent. They also need to be consistent with the plausible attacks on the data. If there are two plausible attacks on the data, they may have two different thresholds respectively that are appropriate.

A methodology needs to provide a process to set these thresholds. Once the threshold(s) are known, then it would be possible to make a case that a data set has an acceptably small re-identification risk.

9. Is there a process and template for the implementation of the re-identification risk assessment and de-identification?

Real world use cases can vary in terms of how de-identification fits within the corporate data flow. For example, if the data custodian is a research registry then there may be an analyst who performs de-identification on a case-by-case basis. On the other hand, a data custodian may be performing de-identification of data feeds on a continuous basis. The implementation of de-identification will be different in each of these two scenarios. The latter, for example, will require some programming effort to integrate de-identification within an automated workflow.

10. Does the methodology provide a set of data transformations to apply?

If the risk of re-identification is deemed to be unacceptably high, then transformations to the data must be performed to reduce the likelihood of re-identification. A methodology should provide a set of transformations that are suitable for the type of data that is being considered. The transformations should also be known to be irreversible or there should be a way to assess whether they can be easily reversed. This latter consideration is important because there are many techniques that have been proposed to protect data, and some of them have been found to be vulnerable or only applicable under certain conditions.

An additional consideration is whether the transformations are acceptable by the end user community. Data transformations that would not be trusted or accepted by a particular end user are not very helpful. This may lead to different sets of data transformations for different data user communities.

11. Does the methodology consider data utility?

Consideration of data utility is an important practical requirement. If a de-identification methodology provides strong privacy protection but produces data sets that are not useful for their intended secondary purposes, then no one will implement it. Data utility can be considered at a subjective level where data users would provide feedback about whether they think the de-identified data is acceptable to them. More objective metrics can also be used to evaluate the extent of information loss after the de-identification has been performed. Objective metrics are particularly useful when different ways to de-identify a data set need to be compared.

Consideration of data utility means that in practice a de-identification methodology will be iterative. A data set may be de-identified but the resultant data utility is not seen as sufficient. Then the de-identification parameters are reset and a different de-identification pass is performed.

12. Does the methodology address de-identification governance?

De-identification governance is an important consideration for all organizations performing de-identification. Governance would cover activities such as: (a) how often does the re-identification risk assessment need to be re-performed, (b) when and which data recipients need to be audited to ensure that they are complying with the conditions for a data release, (c) the regular examination of the disclosures of overlapping data sets to ensure that the re-identification risk for any individual data recipient is not increasing with new data releases, or that potential collusion among data recipients does not increase the re-identification risk, (d) maintaining transparency around the de-identification practices of the organization, (e) assigning responsibility for de-identification, (f) maintaining oversight of changes in relevant regulations and legislation, as well as court cases, (g) a response process in case there has been a re-identification attack, and (h) ensuring that individuals performing de-identification have adequate and up-to-date training.

Summary

If a de-identification methodology meets the above twelve criteria then it will be consistent with existing standards. If it does not meet all twelve criteria then the data custodian is taking a non-trivial risk that an audit or investigation would result in a negative finding.

It should be expected that any analyst applying this methodology would need to have sufficient training. This training would have to be formal, and augmented with practical experience (either through case studies or coaching). Although the training and expertise of the analyst in using the methodology is a requirement that is present in the regulations, we have treated this as separate from the methodology itself.

Scoring

During an assessment of the methodology, the twelve criteria can be scored along two dimensions: implementation and capability. The implementation dimension indicates whether a criterion can be satisfied in any way—it is essentially an indicator of existence of a practice or set of practices. The capability dimension indicates how well a criterion can be satisfied. A criterion can be satisfied in a very basic manner (low capability), or in a very convincing manner (high capability). A criterion must be implemented to have any capability.

A Data Masking Case Study

To illustrate how the criteria of the de-identification methodology work, it is informative to apply them to a case study. The case study I will use is that of a typical data masking methodology. Consider a scenario of a data custodian taking data from a production database and using it for secondary purposes, such as software testing or analytics by the marketing department. The data custodian is considering using a data masking methodology for that purpose. The analysis below in Table 1 is based on our experiences evaluating data masking methodologies across multiple projects. Of course, a particular methodology may score a little better or worse than our general assessment. However, based on the ones that we have seen, it is unlikely that they will veer off too much from the summary below.

As can be seen, seven of the twelve criteria are not met by asking methodologies, two are often met quite well, and three are partially met. This makes clear that a typical masking methodology would not be considered sufficient in terms of being consistent with contemporary de-identification standards. This deficiency presents a challenge to data custodians in that they cannot be assured that such methodologies will produce data sets that would be considered as having a very small risk of re-identification if there is an audit or an investigation.

CRITERION	ASSESSMENT
Is the methodology documented?	Yes—often a data masking methodology will be documented. The documentation is often specific to using a particular data masking tool.
Has the methodology received external or independent scrutiny?	No—we have not seen a masking methodology that has received general scrutiny. The primary reason is that these are often proprietary and therefore there are few opportunities for them to be scrutinized. In some cases a data custodian will bring in a third party to evaluate a masking methodology that they have or intend to implement.

Does the methodology require and have a process for the explicit identification of the data custodian and the data recipients?	To some extent this is performed. IN order to perform masking it is necessary to understand the data flows, although the data flows are not characterized as being from one or more data custodians to one or more data recipients.
Does the methodology require and have a process for the identification of plausible adversaries and plausible attacks on the data?	No—masking methodologies do not have the concept of risk assessment and measurement, and therefore there is no reason to identify adversaries and attacks. There is usually a fixed set of data transformations performed on a fixed set of direct identifiers and quasi-identifiers.
Does the methodology require and have a process for the determination of direct identifiers and quasi-identifiers?	No—the type of de-identification is not a function of the field type and therefore there is no reason to make that distinction. Masking is applied to all of the fields that are selected.
Does the methodology have a process for identifying mitigating controls to manage any residual risks?	No—because masking methodologies do not have a concept of risk assessment and measurement, there is no reason for considering mitigating controls. A fixed set of masking techniques are applied to all selected fields.
Does the methodology require the measurement of actual re-identification risks for different attacks from the data?	No—masking methodologies do not have the concept of an attack as that information would result in adjustments to the masks that are performed.
Is it possible to set, in a defensible way, re-identification risk thresholds?	No—there is no concept of risk assessment and measurement in masking methodologies. Therefore, there is no purpose in defining thresholds.

Is there a process and template for the implementation of the re-identification risk assessment and de-identification?	To some extent masking methodologies will have well defined implementation steps. These would include the integration of masking tools within a data custodian's technical environment. Although that implementation process would not pertain to risk assessment.
Does the methodology provide a set of data transformations to apply?	To some extent this is true. Yes—masking methodologies will provide a number of data transformation options. However, a number of the most commonly used transformations are known to be reversible. Therefore, this criterion is partially met.
Does the methodology consider data utility?	Yes—almost all data masking methodologies will consider data utility. Often data utility drives the type of mask that is applied and which fields are considered in the masking process.
Does the methodology address de-identification governance?	No—because masking is not based on a concept of risk, there is no reason for ongoing governance of the de-identification process.

Table 1: Analysis of Data Masking Methodologies Across Multiple Projects

Relevant Reading on Current De-Identification Standards

- Guidelines from the US Department of Health and Human Services on interpreting the de-identification guidance in the HIPAA Privacy Rule: Guidance Regarding Methods for De-identification of Protected Health Information in Accordance with the Health Insurance Portability and Accountability Act (HIPAA) Privacy Rule.

- Guidance from the UK Information Commissioner's Office: Anonymization: managing data protection risk code of practice.
- Working paper 22: Report on statistical disclosure control, which is a document describing anonymization techniques produced by US federal agencies.
- Checklist on Disclosure Potential of Proposed Data Releases, produced by the Interagency Confidentiality and Data Access Group: An Interest Group of the Federal Committee on Statistical Methodology.
- A Canadian standard developed by the Canadian Institute for Health Information in collaboration with Canada Health Infoway: 'Best Practice' Guidelines for Managing the Disclosure of De-Identified Health Information,

THE "MYTH OF THE PERFECT POPULATION REGISTER" AND RE-IDENTIFICATION RISK ASSESSMENT

Daniel Barth-Jones

Massachusetts Governor William Weld was not feeling well under his cap and gown and he was to about receive an honorary doctorate from Bentley College and then give the commencement address. But, unbeknownst to him, Weld would instead make a crucial contribution to your health information privacy. As Weld stepped forward to the podium, it wasn't what he said that now protects our health privacy, but rather what he did; he collapsed unconscious on the stage shocking the audience and, importantly, drawing substantial media attention.

Weld recovered quickly and the incident might have passed quietly, but for graduate student, Latanya Sweeney, whose graduate studies at MIT had turned her attention to health data released to researchers by the Massachusetts Group Insurance Commission (GIC) with the intention of improving healthcare costs and quality. FTC Senior Privacy Adviser and Law Professor, Paul Ohm, provides a gripping account of Sweeney's famous re-identification of Weld's health insurance data using a Cambridge, MA voter list in his 2010 paper "Broken Promises of Privacy"[9]. Ohm's paper has been frequently cited by those echoing Ohm's claim that computer scientists can purportedly identify individuals hidden within de-identified data with "astonishing ease."

However, the voter list supposedly used to "re-identify" Weld contained only 54,000 residents and Cambridge demographics at the time of the re-identification attempt show that the population was nearly 100,000 persons. So the linkage between the data sources could not have provided definitive evidence of re-identification. The full detail of this methodological flaw underlying the famous Weld/Cambridge re-identification attacks is available in a recently released paper on the Social Science Research Network[1] and presented in an Electronic Health Information Laboratory Webinar[3].

The fatal flaw was the inability to confirm that Weld was indeed the only man with in his Zip Code with his birth date, exposes some critical logic underlying all re-identification attacks. Re-identification attacks require confirmation that purportedly "re-identified" individuals are the only person within both the sample data set being attacked and the larger population possessing a particular set of combined "quasi-identifier" characteristics. The findings from this critical reexamination of the famous Weld re-identification attack indicate that he was quite likely re-identifiable only by virtue of his having been a public figure experiencing a well-publicized hospitalization, rather than there being any actual certainty to his purported re-identification via the Cambridge voter data.

The Myth of the Perfect Population Register

Available evidence suggests that re-identification risks under current HIPAA protections are now well controlled; [4,5]but some important lessons can still be gained from the critical re-examination of the historic Weld attack. This Risky Business article focuses on the much broader implications exposed by the Weld/Cambridge attacks. Namely, that the very same methodological "Myth of the Perfect Population Register" flaws that undermined the certainty of the Weld re-identification will always create far-reaching systemic challenges for all re-identification attempts—a fundamental fact which must be understood by public policy-makers seeking to realistically assess current privacy risks posed by de-identified data: All re-identification attempts face a strong challenge in being able to create a complete and accurate population register.

Even with today's plethora of internet resources and information, online data frequently contains errors and some people (and/or data elements related to them) will always be missing with any easily obtained source of data. The reality facing a would-be data intruder (i.e., a person attempting re-identification) is that in addition to frequent errors in online information, people move (and don't always promptly update their address information); and some segment of any population is simply "off the grid". Consistency problems, such as differences in data coding between data sets, real changes in variable values which occur over time for time-dynamic variables and even plain-and-simple keystroke errors all lead to "data divergence".[2]

Admittedly, some sophisticated data intruders might make use of probabilistic data linkage methods which may overcome some limited types of these data errors, but such probabilistic linkage is inherently subject to uncertainty. Furthermore, real world data intruders would rarely, if ever, be in a position to test and verify the extent of this potentially substantial uncertainty.

Why Disclosure Risk Scientists Routinely and Intentionally Overestimate Re-identification Risks

In fact, a somewhat furtive "insider" trade secret underlies most similar work conducted by disclosure risk scientists. The same "perfect population register" Achilles heel that limited the accuracy of the Weld re-identification underlies many, if not most, of the re-identification risk estimates made by statistical disclosure risk scientists. The problem is that creating a "perfect population register"—one that is complete and accurate is a tremendous challenge for even the U.S. Census Bureau and would typically be far beyond the likely abilities of a hypothetical data intruder. Not surprisingly, disclosure risk scientists themselves cannot afford to complete this final exhaustive step when making their re-identification risk estimates. So they wisely skip this last essential task and instead make easily obtained, but highly conservative, estimates of the true re-identification risks.

The estimates are conservative because they often involved assuming that a perfect population register could be constructed, when, in fact, this simply is not possible. This overly conservative estimation is an entirely appropriate practice as long as everyone who interprets these results understands that we've left out the hardest part of the equation and chosen to err strongly on the side of caution in order to protect privacy. It needs to be recognized though that missing and incorrect data will inevitably plague any attempt to build a perfect population register and, thus, to the extent the population register is imperfect, significant proportions of purported "re-identification" matches may simply be incorrect.

For example, in the United States it has consistently been the case for some time that roughly 29 percent of the voting age population is not registered to vote;[7] and as explained in some detail in my recent paper[1], not only are each of these non-voters directly protected from re-identification attempts using voter registers—but, they also importantly confound attempts to re-identify those registered to vote whenever such incomplete voter registers are used. When just a single person sharing the quasi-identifier characteristics with a purported re-identification victim is missing from the voter register, then the probability of a correct re-identification for this target is only 50%.

It seems only prudent to routinely presume that data intruders could be able to create near-perfect population registers for small or isolated populations for limited time periods particularly when aided by their personal knowledge of the population within a specific location.[6] But because the final step in the re-identification process always depends critically on being able to rule out that there are not individuals missing from the population register and that the quasi-identifier information was correct in both the data source and the population register, every certain re-identification faces the same dauntingly effort-intensive and often very expensive prerequisites.

Even with the continuing expansion of available online information resources and commercial "Fourth Bureau" agencies aiding the construction of population registers, any realistic assessment of a lone data intruder's ability to accurately and affordably create perfect (or near perfect) population registers which include time dynamic quasi-identifiers (such as patient locations) for populations numbering in the tens of thousands should include some healthy skepticism about the purported "re-identifications". Fortunately, the mundane challenges of maintaining high quality and timely data are great allies in our fight against re-identification risks. So, just like attempting to confirm that there are "no black swans", it is clear that it is a tall order indeed to verify supposed re-identifications with anything approaching certainty in very large populations.

Professor Ohm has written another very compelling and remarkably astute paper cautioning public policy makers to beware of the "Myth of the Superuser".[8] Ohm's point with regard to this mythical "Superuser" is not that such Superusers—just substitute "Data Intruders" for our interests' here-do not exist. Ohm isn't even trying to imply that the considerable skills needed to facilitate their attacks are mythical. Rather, Ohm is making the point that by inappropriately conflating the rare and anecdotal accomplishments of notorious hackers with the actions of typical users we unwittingly form highly distorted views of the normative behavior which is under consideration for regulatory control. This misdirected focus leads to poorly constructed public policy and unintended consequences. It's not hard to see that extremely important parallels exist here with regard to *"Myth of the Perfect Population Register"*.

The inability of most data intruders to construct accurate and complete population registers capable of supporting re-identification attacks has wide reaching implications. The most important of which show how seriously we should take Ohm's own claims about the "astonishing ease" of re-identification. As I've written in a previous paper coauthored with University of Arizona Law Professor, Jane Bambauer Yakowitz,[10]

For this very same reason, oft-repeated apprehensions that evolving re-identification risks arising from new data sources like Facebook or new technologies will rapidly out-pace our abilities to recognize and appropriately respond with effective de-identification methods are unfounded. It is simply not the case that re-identification methods can be easily automated and rapidly spread via the Internet as some have mistakenly asserted. The Myth of the Perfect Population Register assures us that confident re-identifications will always require labor intensive efforts spent building and confirming high quality, time-specific population registers. Re-identification lacks the easy transmission and transferability of computer viruses or other computer security vulnerabilities.

It will never become the domain of hacker "script kiddies" because of the competing "limits of human bandwidth" discussed in Ohm's Superuser paper. Careful consideration of Ohm's Superuser arguments coupled with the Myth of the Perfect Population Register lead us to the conclusion that re-identification attempts will continue to be expensive and time-consuming to conduct, require serious data management and statistical skills to execute, rarely be successful when data has been properly de-identified, and, most importantly, almost always turn out to be ultimately uncertain as to whether any purported re-identifications have actually been correct.

Definitions

Quasi-Identifiers—Quasi-identifiers are fields that can also identify individuals but are also useful for data analysis. Examples of these include dates, demographic information (such as race and ethnicity), and socioeconomic variables.

References

1. Daniel C. Barth-Jones, *The 'Re-Identification' of Governor William Weld's Medical Information: A Critical Re-Examination of Health Data Identification Risks and Privacy Protections, Then and Now* (June 4, 2012). Available at SSRN: http://ssrn.com/abstract=2076397 or http://dx.doi.org/10.2139/ssrn.2076397

2. George T. Duncan, Mark Elliott, Juan-Jose Salazar-González, *Statistical Confidentiality: Principles and Practice*. Springer. 2011, p. 39-40

3. Daniel C. Barth-Jones,. *A Critical Examination of Pre-and-Post HIPAA Re-identification Risks. Electronic Health Information Laboratory Webinar*. Delivered July 18, 2012. (https://www.ehealthinformation.ca/survey/webinarjul182012.aspx)

4. Khaled El Emam, Elizabeth Jonker, Luk Arbuckle, Bradley Malin. *A Systematic Review of Re-Identification Attacks on Health Data*. PLoS One 2011; Vol 6(12):e28071.

5. Khaled El Emam, Elizabeth Jonker, Anita Fineberg.: *The Case for De-identifying Personal Health Information*. Electronic Health Information Laboratory, Children's Hospital of Eastern Ontario Research Institute, Ottawa, Canada, 2011. http://papers.ssrn.com/sol3/papers.cfm?abstract_id=1744038

6. Mark Elliot, Angela Dale, *Scenarios of attack: the data intruder's perspective on statistical disclosure risk*. In Netherlands Official Statistics, Volume 14, Spring 1999, Special issue: Statistical disclosure control, p. 6-10.

7. Thom File, Sarah Crissy, *Voting and Registration in the Election of November 2008: Population Characteristics*. U.S. Census Current Population Reports, Issued May 2010. http://www.census.gov/prod/2010pubs/p20-562.pdf

8. Paul Ohm, *The Myth of the Superuser: Fear, Risk, and Harm Online*. U of Colorado Law Legal Studies Research Paper No. 07-14; UC Davis Law Review Vol. 41, No. 4, Page 1327, April 2008. Available at SSRN: http://ssrn.com/abstract=967372.

9. Paul Ohm, *Broken Promises of Privacy: Responding to the Surprising Failure of Anonymization* (August 13, 2009). UCLA Law Review, Vol. 57, p. 1701, 2010; U of Colorado Law Legal Studies Research Paper No. 9-12. Available at SSRN: http://ssrn.com/abstract=1450006.

10. Jane Yakowitz, Daniel C. Barth-Jones,. *The Illusory Privacy Problem in Sorrell v. IMS Health*. 2011. Technology Policy Institute, http://www.techpolicyinstitute.org/files/the%20illusory%20privacy%20problem%20in%20sorrell1.pdf, (accessed 3 Jul 2012

SECTION V

Big Data and Open Data

REALIZING THE PROMISE OF OPEN DATA: AN EXAMPLE OF THE CANADIAN DISCHARGE ABSTRACT DATABASE

Jay Innes

Governments in North America have committed themselves to open data. This means that they will make more of their data available to the public. This is expected to encourage innovations using the data including the creation of new applications that "mash-up" or link multiple data sets in ways that benefit the public. This commitment is also expected to serve as the catalyst for the development of new business models and lead to new insights from data scientists. Of course, open data also promotes transparency in government.

But, when it comes to health data, open data presents some challenges with privacy. If health data is made publicly available then there is the risk that individuals will be identified and their most sensitive health details will be exposed to the world. This is why strong privacy guarantees are needed.

In their published study,[1] El Emam et al. demonstrate how to perform the de-identification on large and complex data sets and prepare it for public release. The report is the culmination of a project examining the key issues related to the creation of a public use microdata file (PUMF). Led by Dr. El Emam, the CEO of Privacy Analytics and the Canada research chair in Electronic Health Information at the University of Ottawa, the project involved conducting various risk assessments to de-identify a sample of 10 percent of all records in a national hospital discharge abstract database (DAD). The data used for the study involved the DAD and was collected by the Canadian Institute for Health Information containing demographic and diagnosis data on more than two million hospital visits for 2008-09.

Amongst many applications, discharge abstract data has been used for public health purposes, including the surveillance of injuries and disease and quality assessments of health-care services. Making discharge abstract data publicly available will benefit many constituencies, including policymakers, researchers, students, and statisticians.

The report offers a primer on PUMFs: defining and categorizing the different types of identification variables and providing information on the different types of re-identification attacks. Helpful strategies provided include the steps required to create a prototype PUMF and the trade-offs to be considered when making data available.

To maximize the application of the data, two different public-use microdata files were produced, and several different risk thresholds were used to provide comparisons on the amount of data generated so users can apply the appropriate level of risk in different circumstances. Analysts and data custodian experts were consulted throughout the project to ensure the accuracy and relevancy of the processes and to promote acceptability of the PUMF among the individuals who work with the data.

In the course of conducting the project, Dr. El Emam and team developed a new algorithm and empirically showed its impact in reducing the amount of data suppression. The outcome is increased data precision, great news for statisticians who covet every detail. It was also revealed that the new suppression algorithm results in less information loss than other traditional approaches that are used to subdue data and protect privacy.

The report provides an understanding of the precision of data that can be achieved at various thresholds while still respecting different privacy guidelines and concludes that a PUMF can be created that will protect against re-identification risk while generating data that is useful to researchers and analysts.

"Worries about privacy are simply not a convincing excuse anymore for not sharing valuable health information as it's largely a solvable problem," says Dr. El Emam, emphasizing that the report also serves as a catalyst to the development of novel data modeling and data-mining techniques.

References

1.   Khaled El Emam, David Paton, Fida Dankar, and Gunes Koru, "De-Identifying a Public Use Microdata File from the Canadian National Discharge Abstract Database," BMC Medical Informatics and Decision Making August, 23, 2011.

BENEFITING FROM BIG DATA WHILE PROTECTING INDIVIDUAL PRIVACY

Khaled El Emam

Most people would agree we are entering the age of "big data." This is a time where large amounts of data from multiple sources are being collected and linked to perform sophisticated analytics for many different purposes. The data tends to be personal, in that it characterizes individual human behaviors and conditions such as their Internet surfing patterns, purchasing behavior in stores, individual health information, details on financial transactions, and physical movements, to name just a few examples. All this personal information, especially when combined, paints a detailed picture about individuals: their likes and dislikes; what they do; and when and where they do it.

Many discussions about big data center around the technology that is needed to process such large volumes of information. Our traditional data management and data processing tools cannot handle the large volumes of data that are being collected. Therefore, completely new systems and algorithms are being developed to process big data efficiently and accurately to "find the signal in the noise." Particular challenges include extracting information from unstructured data (e.g., free-form text instead of fields in a database), and linking data from multiple sources accurately to obtain detailed profiles about individuals.

The analytics performed on big data can be beneficial to the individuals themselves, and to society as a whole. For example, analytics can recommend to individuals, products they may be interested in and may need. Similarly, analytics on linked health data may identify interventions that are beneficial to people with a particular disease or condition, or detect adverse drug events that are serious and warrant removing a drug from the market or restricting the indications for a drug or device.

One of the questions that comes up when we talk about big data is, where does all of this information come from in the first place? Some of it is customer data collected by the various organizations that are providing different products and services. Another large source of data is freely available online as individuals provide more details about their lives and interests on social-networking sites, on blogs, and in their "tweets" (via Twitter). In some cases, it is possible to buy individual-level data, for example, about magazine subscriptions or financial transactions. Government registries also provide useful information, such as date of birth information and data on things such as liens. Aggregate or summary data (e.g., averages or percentages) can be helpful for this kind of analytics as well. For example, by just knowing an individual's zip or postal code, it is possible to get a good estimate of an individual's income, level of education, and number of children using just aggregate data.

Existing legal frameworks allow the collection, use, and disclosure of personal information as long as it is de-identified (or anonymized) and there is no requirement to obtain individuals' consent if this is the case. However, the de-identification not only applies to original data, it also applies to data that has been linked with other information. Therefore, as different data sources are integrated, there is a constant need to evaluate identifiability to ensure that the risk of re-identification remains acceptably low.

One advantage of having lots of data, or big data, to analyze is that it makes de-identification easier to achieve. The reason is that there is a greater likelihood there are more similar people in a big data set than in a smaller one. By definition, smaller data sets are more challenging to manage from an identifiability perspective because it is easier to be unique in smaller databases.

In order to more fully understand the nuances around de-identification practice and de-identification regulations, it is important to understand the distinction between "identity disclosure" and "attribute disclosure." Privacy laws only regulate identity disclosure, which is when the identity of an individual can be determined by examining a database. For example, if an "adversary" is someone who tries to re-identify a record in the data set and can determine that record number 7 belongs to Bob Smith, then this would be considered "identity disclosure" because the identity of record number 7 is now known to be Bob's.

"Attribute disclosure" is less straightforward to understand, but this example, pertaining to vaccination of teenage girls against HPV (the human papillomavirus, a virus believed to cause cervical cancer) should serve this purpose. If someone were to perform some analysis on an HPV data set that included information on religious affiliation, he or she might discover that most people of religion "A" do not vaccinate their teenage daughters against HPV, because HPV is correlated with sexual activity and therefore argue they do not need it, then this is an example of "attribute disclosure." Here we discover that a particular group, characterized by their religion, in this instance, has a particular attribute or behavior. Although no individual records in the database were identified, if it is known that Bob Smith follows religion "A," one can learn something new about him whether he is in the database or not.

We can generalize this example to, say, retail. From analyzing a large retail database linked with a magazine subscription list, we can discover that the majority of forty-year-old women who are stay-at-home moms in zip code 12345 like tea, read a particular type of magazine, and have a particular political affiliation. This conclusion does not identify any individuals, but we are still able to come to certain conclusions about these women and their lifestyles. With this information, it is possible to precisely target advertisements to these women, even though no one's identity was revealed to draw a conclusion from the database.

As mentioned, privacy laws do not regulate attribute disclosure. Therefore, drawing inferences from databases is still a valid exercise, as long as the original data and any linked data sets are convincingly de-identified. In fact, an examination of the evidence on real-world identification attacks reveals that they are all "identity disclosure," which is the main type of attack one needs to pragmatically protect against. But to address concerns about such "attribute disclosure" inferences, transparency is important. By transparency, I mean letting the individuals know what data is being collected about them, what data is being linked or would possibly be linked to it, and how it is being used. Giving individuals in a database an opt-out option would not be practical because the data would already be de-identified.

WHO'S AFRAID OF BIG DATA?

Khaled El Emam

I recently attended a number of presentations on Big Data. Much of the discussions at those events were about the potential benefits of Big Data and the really impressive ways the "fire hose" of information can be used to benefit communities and create wealth.

For example, one application "crawls" the vast amounts of unstructured data on websites including online news publications, social-media sites like Twitter, government websites, blogs, and financial databases to predict where and when riots and protests will likely occur. They have "public" as well as commercial data they access. Their solution is targeted at defense and intelligence, corporate security, financial services, and competitive intelligence markets.

Another application monitors location and communications using mobile phones to model patterns of formal and informal interactions among employees. Yet another posts short message service (SMS) numbers on products in supermarkets and stores, and when people send a message, they are given a credit on their phone bill. But now the product company knows who purchased their product from their phone number and can link that with other demographic and socioeconomic data to develop a precise profile of their customers.

Another common theme at the presentations was that "people have already given up their privacy" and "the benefits are so great, privacy does not matter." There did not seem to be a general understanding of the privacy risks from Big Data or that they need to be handled. While my sample is clearly not representative, these beliefs are a recurring pattern, from my observations. I will therefore highlight four reasons the Big Data community needs to care about privacy.

As masses of information are taken from disparate sources and mashed together to produce the desired data set, the chances of identifying individuals and breaching their privacy becomes more and more possible. People are only now really paying attention to privacy because of the increasing amount of coverage by the media of companies like Facebook and their use of personal data. With this coverage, people are now becoming leery about the data they share online about themselves. Individuals are creating accounts with fake names and dates of birth. In terms of health care, surveys indicate a nontrivial and increasing percentage of patients are lying to their doctors and omitting important details from their medical histories. Ultimately, the problem that arises with this type of practice is that the value in the data is diluted. We are no longer left with accurate information to analyze.

Organizations that are caught collecting more personal data than is necessary to provide a service or are disclosing personal information become "creepy"; some consumers avoid continuing doing business with them, or continue reluctantly. Being known as the creepy guy in the room is not a good basis for growing a business or maintaining a consumer relationship based on analytics on their data.

By collecting personal data, organizations are also at risk of data breaches. Covered entities in the United States, which are expected to follow the practices in the HIPAA Security Rule, have an annual breach rate exceeding 25 percent based on recent estimates. The costs of a breach of personal information are amplified when there are breach notification laws, as is the case in most states and in some Canadian jurisdictions. Breach notification costs include those from the notification itself, remedial action, litigation, lost business, and regulator penalties. These have been estimated to amount from $200 to $300 per individual affected by the breach.

Finally, regulators are weighing in more heavily on the subject of privacy. Without paying strong attention to the privacy question, stricter regulations (or legislation) will be implemented and enforced. The regulations will put limits on the collection, use, and disclosure of personal information. The extent of restrictions will, at least partially, be a function of the perceived abuses of privacy that become publicly known.

In summary, we need to tread carefully with privacy and ensure best practices are used. One of these best practices will be to de-identify data at the earliest opportunity. But this will not be the only best practice. Good governance and transparency, including some assurance against "stigmatizing analytics" will be necessary. These are the types of analytics that stigmatize individuals and affect their life opportunities, like getting a job or getting insured.

SECTION VI

Tools

DATA MASKING WITH PARAT

Grant Middleton

Introduction

The Privacy Analytics Risk Assessment Tool (PARAT), used in masking and de-identification, is available from Privacy Analytics. It provides a multitude of functionalities that can be used throughout the entire masking and de-identification process, from database management, to risk assessments and de-identification.

One part to this set of functionality is the data-masking tool (DMT). The DMT provides an additional layer of data transformation capabilities to PARAT. Whereas PARAT's data de-identification was previously focused on quasi-identifiers, the DMT allows a user to handle the direct identifiers within a data set. Direct identifiers such as first and last names, social security numbers, medical record numbers, facility names, and many more can be transformed using the DMT.

In many situations, the direct identifiers will not be the focus of any analytics. This means they can be transformed into random values or redacted without any loss of data utility. This process is called masking. One would not mask the fields that would be used for data analysis—instead, the de-identification functions of PARAT should be used for those.

Some examples of data-masking-use cases are (a) creating a data set from production databases that will be used for software testing; (b) creating a clinical data set that will be used to conduct demonstrations by the sales team of an IT system; and (c) creating data sets that can be used for training on a clinical system.

Throughout the rest of this article, we will show you how the DMT can be used to help mask a set of patient data. Our focus today will be on a simple cross-sectional data set.

The Data

We will be working with a single patient data set that contains the following fields:

Field	Data Type	Mask?
ID	Integer	No
Given Name	Text	Yes
Surname	Text	Yes
Initials	Text	Yes
Title	Text	Yes
Birth City	Text	Yes
Birth Country	Text	Yes
Birth Date	Date	No
Ethnicity	Text	No
Gender	Text	No
Race	Text	No
SSN	Text	Yes
Birth State	Text	Yes

Table 1: Single Patient Data Set

All direct identifiers have been marked for masking. The ID field and the quasi-identifiers have not been marked for masking.

170

We do this because we want to retain the quasi-identifier data for PARAT de-identification. In a future article I will address the issue of creating pseudonyms using PARAT, which is the proper way to handle the ID field.

Getting Started

To open the DMT, select the "Masking Tool" item under the "Database Masking" menu (Figure 1). This will open the DMT in a separate window.

Figure 1: Masking Tool Menu

Basic Data-Masking Settings

Then specify the masking settings to describe to the DMT how to mask our data. Figure 2 highlights all of the important areas of the DMT.

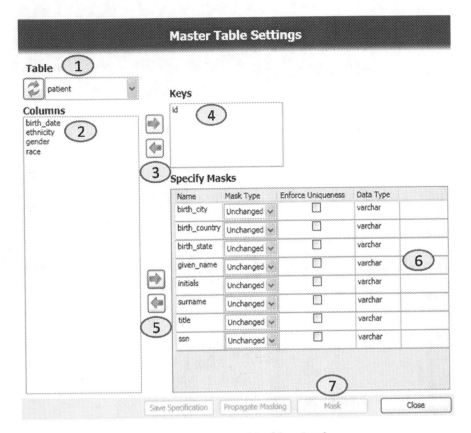

Figure 2: Basic Data-Masking Settings

1. Table Selection—To select the data set that you want to mask, use the table drop-down menu and select the appropriate table
2. Columns Section—The columns section lists all of the fields that are found within the data set. One or more fields can be selected with the mouse.
3. Key Field Movement Arrows—If you would like to specify a key, these arrows can be used to move a field from the columns section to the keys section.
4. Keys Section—The keys section lists all of the keys that have been defined for this data set. Here we have specified the "ID" field as a key.

172

5. Mask Field Movement Arrows—These arrows allow fields to be moved from the columns section to the masking specification section.
6. Masking Specification Section—This section is where the masks are defined. We have moved the eight fields marked for masking to the masking specification section using the mask field movement arrows.
7. Mask Buttons—These buttons are used to start the masking process, save the settings, or close the window.

Specifying the Masks

After we specify the basic masking settings, we need to specify the masks that we would like to apply to the data. For each column in the specify masks section, we select the mask type from the "Mask Type" drop-down list.

If the mask can be customized, a "Format" text box will appear with instructions on how to specify the custom formatting. We have specified custom masks for both the "initials" and "title" fields since there is no predefined mask type for these fields.

To ensure that each value is uniquely masked, enable the "Enforce Uniqueness" checkbox. This is useful for fields like social security numbers where each value must be unique to an individual. We have enabled the "Enforce Uniqueness" checkbox for the "ssn" field.

Specify Masks

Name	Mask Type	Enforce Uniqueness	Data Type
birth_city	City	☐	varchar
birth_country	Country	☐	varchar
birth_state	State	☐	varchar
given_name	First Name	☐	varchar
initials	Custom	☐	varchar
Format: @@		@ = random letter, # = random number, any other character will be left unchanged.	
surname	Last Name	☐	varchar
title	Custom	☐	varchar
Format: @@@@		@ = random letter, # = random number, any other character will be left unchanged.	
ssn	SSN	☑	varchar

Figure 3: Specify Masks

When all the mask settings are correct, the masking operation can be started by clicking the "Mask" button.

Result

Figure 4 shows the pre-masking data for four different patient records. Figure 5 shows the post-masking data for the same patients. The ID field has been left unchanged and can be used to compare the two data sets. We can see that each of the post-masking patient records has been de-identified and no longer resemble the pre-masking records.

id	given_name	surname	initials	title	birth_city	birth_country	ssn	birth_state
546890	Eric	Davis	A	Mr.	Cincinnati	United States	180-10-0662	Ohio
3524774	James	Lee	E	Mr.	Minneapolis	United States	306-10-2429	Minnesota
3564808	Kylie	Cox	O	Mrs.	Fresno	United States	347-10-6463	California
4526877	Faith	Hall	A	Mrs.	North Hempstead	United States	510-10-2693	New York

Figure 4: Pre-Masking Data

174

id	given_name	surname	initials	title	birth_city	birth_country	ssn	birth_state
546890	Kilby	Neer	PG	FHXK	Rock Mills	Qatar	224-164-627	WI
3524774	Pearl	Smallwood	IR	JNGU	Augusta	Sweden	340-899-192	AK
3564808	Ann	Dymond	IV	ZYHP	Blomkest	Macedonia	279-454-416	IA
4526877	Connell	Kentle	PM	AAKB	Leon	Switzerland	174-155-414	PA

Figure 5: Post-Masking Data

Performance

The DMT has been shown to work on very large data sets—both with many records and many columns. Table 2 below provides some performance results.

Conclusions

The DMT adds robustness to PARAT's ability to mask data, and mitigate risk, by including the ability to mask direct identifiers.

This functionality, in addition to PARAT's industry-leading de-identification of quasi-identifiers allows data custodians to create complete clinical data sets while maintaining privacy, and still retain significant utility by separating the transformations to direct identifiers and quasi-identifiers.

# of Records	# of Masked Columns	Total Time (HH:MM:SS)
250,000	20	00:02:00
600,000	5	00:00:39
20,000,000	5	00:05:52
100,000,000	1	00:11:00
100,000,000	4	00:21:00

Table 2: Performance results of DMT

PARAT FUNCTIONALITY: MAINTAINING INTEGRITY WHEN MASKING A MULTI-TABLE DATA SET

Grant Middleton

Introduction

In my last article, "PARAT Functionality: Data Masking," I introduced PARAT's masking functionality as a tool to help protect a data set. The primary masking technique used in PARAT is randomization, which provides strong assurances that the masked values cannot be reversed back to their original values. Masking is applied on "direct identifiers" in a database, which are the fields that can directly identify individuals, such as their name, social security number (SSN), and e-mail address. Sometimes it is also necessary to mask fields that may not be so much direct identifiers but fields that can lead to fraud and (medical) identity theft. For example, in Ontario the provincial health insurance number would be difficult to use to re-identify an individual by itself, nevertheless, if it ends up in the wrong hands, it can result in insurance fraud and possibly identity theft. Furthermore, in Ontario there are strong legal restrictions on the collection, use, and disclosure of health insurance numbers.

In this article, I will expand on PARAT's data-masking capabilities by discussing the data-masking propagation feature of PARAT. One of the challenges associated with masking is how to maintain integrity across multiple tables in a relational database. If "Mike Smith" is masked to "John Simpson" in one table, we will also want Mike Smith to be masked to John Simpson across all other tables in the data set. Maintaining this integrity helps preserve more of the utility of the data set.

PARAT's data-masking tool (DMT) allows users to propagate masking throughout multiple tables, ensuring integrity can be maintained throughout the database. A basic concept in this propagation is that of a "master" table and a "child" table. A master table is where the primary masking occurs, and a child table is one that needs to inherit the masked values from the master table to ensure consistency.

I will use as an example the propagation of a name. But this can be easily extended to, for example, an SSN.

The Data Set

We will use two different tables to demonstrate DMT masking propagation: an inpatient claims table (Table 1) and an outpatient claims table (Table 2). The inpatient claims table contains patient demographics as well as drug, procedure, and monetary claims data. The outpatient claims table contains patient demographics, as well as diagnosis, procedure, and monetary claims data. Both tables contain a Medical Record Number (MRN) field that can be used to link the same patients from each table.

Field	Data Type	Mask?
MRN	Integer	No
First Name	Text	Yes
Last Name	Text	Yes
Sex	Text	No
Date of Birth	Text	No
Zip Code	Text	No
SSN	Text	Yes
E-mail	Text	Yes
Base DRG Code	Integer	No
ICD9 PRCDR Code	Integer	No
Length of Stay	Integer	No
Quintile Payment Average	Integer	No
Quintile Payment Code	Integer	No

Table 1: Inpatient Claims Data Set

Field	Data Type	Mask?
MRN	Integer	No
First Name	Text	Yes
Last Name	Text	Yes
Sex	Text	No
Date of Birth	Date	No
Zip Code	Text	No
SSN	Text	Yes
Email	Text	Yes
ICD9 Diagnosis Code	Integer	No
HCPCS Procedure Code	Integer	No
Medicare Payment	Integer	No
Count of services	Integer	No

Table 2: Outpatient Claims Dataset

Masking is only done on direct identifiers in a data set. Quasi-identifiers (QIs) are usually not masked since they contain data that are useful for analytics purposes. In general, masking will distort the data in ways that make it harder to analyze. Therefore, for the QIs that will be analyzed, a whole different set of de-identification techniques need to be used to maximize data utility. In a future article, I will illustrate some of these de-identification capabilities in PARAT.

In our current example, the MRN field and QIs have not been marked for masking. In situations where the MRN could be used to link these records with other patient data sets, it would likely be a requirement that the MRN field also be masked. For this example we will assume the MRN field does not link with any other data sets.

Getting Started

To open the DMT, select the Masking Tool item under the Database Masking menu (Figure 1). This will open the DMT in a separate window.

Figure 1: Masking Tool Menu

Master Table Settings

Here we specify the settings for the master table (Inpatient Claims).

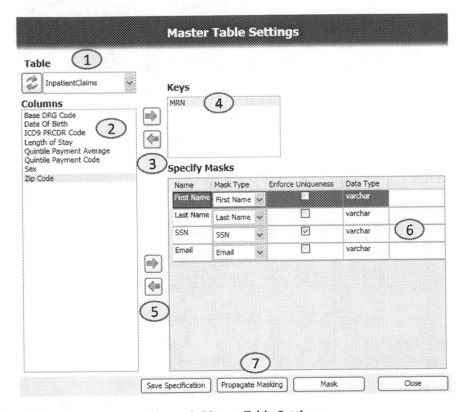

Figure 2: Master Table Settings

1. Table Selection—Use the table drop-down menu and select the Inpatient Claims table.
2. Columns Section—Select the specific columns you would like to move (either the key or the QIs).
3. Key Field Movement Arrows—Use the arrows to move the selected columns to the Keys section.
4. Keys Section—The Keys section lists all the keys that have been defined for this data set. Here we have specified the MRN field as a key.
5. Mask Field Movement Arrows—Use the arrows to move the selected columns to the Masking Specification section.
6. Masking Specification Section—Here we specify the masks for each field (first name, last name, SSN, and e-mail, respectively).

7. Propagate Masking Button—We use this button to load the child table settings.

Child Table Settings

Here we specify the relationship between the parent table (Inpatient Claims) and the child table(s) (Outpatient Claims).

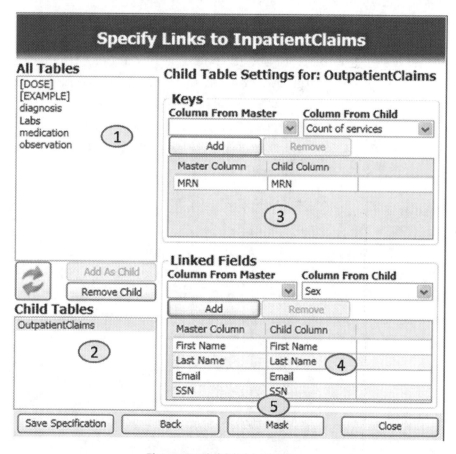

Figure 3: Child Table Settings

1. Table List—Here we are able to select the tables that we would like to add as child tables.

2. Child Tables—Here are the list of specified child tables. We have selected Outpatient Claims.

3. Keys—This section is dependent on the child table that is selected. Here you specify the key relationship between the parent and child table. Here the MRN field is matched from the parent to child.

4. Linked Fields—Here you specify the fields that are linked together and therefore will be masked using the mask specified in the master table settings. In this example we have matched the first name, last name, SSN, and e-mail fields. You do not have to match all of the parent fields to a child field. You only need to select the fields you want to propagate.

5. Mask Button—Once all the master-to-child table relationships have been specified, we click the mask button to perform the masking.

Results

Figure 4 shows a partial view of the Inpatient data set before and after masking. Figure 5 shows a partial view of the Outpatient data set before and after masking. Patients with the MRN 6 and 15 can be found in both the Inpatient and Outpatient tables. These two patients are still identical across the two tables.

MRN	First Name	Last Name	Sex	Date Of Birth	Zip Code	SSN	Email
6	Belle	Rainey	f	16/09/1938 0:00	30055	108-717-215	Belle.Rainey@Atwater.com
11	Algernon	Armand	m	03/08/1935 0:00	43768	806-505-275	Algernon.Armand@Cliff.com
15	Hope	Levan	f	25/02/1931 0:00	28632	532-093-078	Hope.Levan@Moira.com
26	Frederick	Martyk	m	10/04/1928 0:00	63312	309-595-051	Frederick.Martyk@Merle.com

MRN	First Name	Last Name	Sex	Date Of Birth	Zip Code	SSN	Email
6	Jennifer	Honey	f	16/09/1938 0:00	30055	583-675-063	Bret@Leonard.com
11	Gideon	Hartzberger	m	03/08/1935 0:00	43768	525-081-523	Helen@Eliot.com
15	Shelley	Kopacz	f	25/02/1931 0:00	28832	225-489-180	Charity@Brina.com
26	Felicia	Ditta	m	10/04/1928 0:00	63312	933-314-246	Diana@Zachariah.com

Figure 4: Inpatient Claims Before and After

MRN	First Name	Last Name	Sex	Date Of Birth	Zip Code	SSN	Email
5	Normand	Moeller	m	29/04/1937 0:00	4890	422-305-149	Darell@Griswald.com
6	Belle	Rainey	f	16/09/1938 0:00	30055	108-717-215	Belle.Rainey@Atwater.com
15	Hope	Levan	f	25/02/1931 0:00	28832	532-093-078	Hope.Levan@Moira.com
44	Ely	Zoney	m	01/07/1940 0:00	39931	765-784-743	Ely.Zoney@Landon.com

MRN	First Name	Last Name	Sex	Date Of Birth	Zip Code	SSN	Email
5	Clay	Keith	m	29/04/1937 0:00	4890	471-190-407	Leroy@Basil.com
6	Jennifer	Honey	f	16/09/1938 0:00	30055	583-675-088	Bret@Leonard.com
15	Shelley	Kopacz	f	25/02/1931 0:00	28832	225-489-180	Charity@Brina.com
44	Brent	Pacheco	m	01/07/1940 0:00	39931	397-510-560	Allan@Joy.com

Figure 5: Outpatient Claims Before and After

In this example we used the primary key, the MRN field, to find matching patients across both tables. However, masking propagation is not reliant on a primary key to find matching records. The DMT can perform masking propagation based solely on the individual values within a field. The resulting data set would be slightly different since individual values, regardless of the primary key, would be masked to the same values.

Conclusion

In this article, we have shown how PARAT DMT can be used to propagate masking across tables. To achieve this, DMT requires the user to specify:

1. The parent and child tables;
2. An optional key that links records across the tables;
3. A set of identifiers to be masked, as well as the type of masking to be applied to these fields; and
4. A mapping of the relationships between the parent and child fields.
5. The result is a new data set with masked data that maintains the integrity of the original data set.

PARAT FUNCTIONALITY: CONTINUOUS AND BATCH DE-IDENTIFICATION WITH PARAT

Grant Middleton

Introduction

There are a number of use cases where it is necessary to perform masking and de-identification in batch mode either once or on a continuous basis. Some examples are:

- An organization needs to disclose data on a monthly or quarterly basis. Even though the fields are the same, each release contains new records about new patients. To ensure consistency for these regular data disclosures, it is necessary to run the same masking and de-identification process each time. This consistent process would also be documented in the data-sharing agreement or contract that covers the disclosure.

- A public health program is collecting data from sites across the country on a regular basis. All the data is going into a single de-identified data repository. To ensure that all of the source data is de-identified in exactly the same way, they all need to run masking and de-identification using exactly the same parameters.
- An organization is pulling data regularly from its medical devices deployed at hospitals across the country. This data is then masked and de-identified and provided to the software testing team on a quarterly basis. The testing team uses it to ensure that future releases of their software for these devices are functioning and can perform with the up-to-date real data.
- An analyst wants to examine the impact on her data from de-identification using different parameters. She does not want to point and click a large number of times to perform a simulation but wants to create a batch simulation job that will extract multiple data (say through sampling), de-identify them using various parameters, and then quickly export them.

All of these scenarios require a capability to perform masking and de-identification in batch mode. In this article I will explain the capabilities in PARAT for batch processing and how to perform unattended continuous masking and de-identification.

Specification Files

PARAT uses specification files to automatically execute specific actions such as importing or de-identifying a data set. These files are created within PARAT, are XML-based, and contain the settings that are used by PARAT to perform the action. For example, a de-identification specification file will contain the risk threshold, quasi-identifiers, hierarchies, weights, and other settings that will be used to de-identify a data set.

There are seven different types of specification files:

1. CSV import
2. CSV export
3. Database import
4. Database export
5. De-identification (risk mitigation)
6. Masking
7. SQL scripts

Creating Specification Files

Here I will show you how to create each type of specification file. Each type of specification file, with the exception of SQL scripts, is created within PARAT. SQL scripts are manually generated by inserting SQL queries within simple XML tags.

To create a CSV import\export specification file, first perform a CSV import\export. When the import\export is complete, you will have the chance to save the specification file using the "Save Data Specs" button (Figure 1). After saving the specification file it can be used to repeat the import\export on CSV files that contains the same fields.

Figure 1: Save Data Spec for CSV Import

Similarly, to generate a database import export specification file, perform a database import\export using the Database Import\ Export Wizard. When the import\export is complete, you will have the option to save the specification file using the "Save Specs" button (Figure 2).

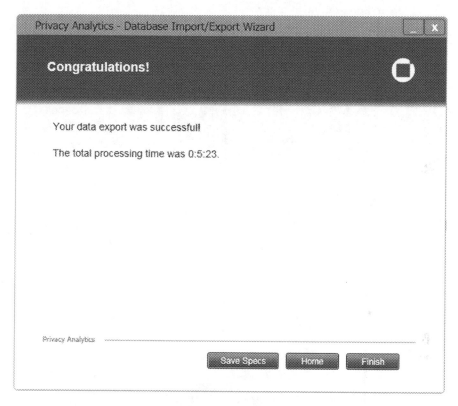

Figure 2: Save Specification for Database Import\Export

To generate a de-identification specification file you need to perform a de-identification on a data set. When the de-identification is complete, you will have the option to save the specification file using the "Save Specification" button (Figure 3). This specification file will work like a manual de-identification, using the same hierarchies that PARAT used during the current de-identification. This specification file allows you to repeat the exact same de-identification on any other data set that contains the same fields.

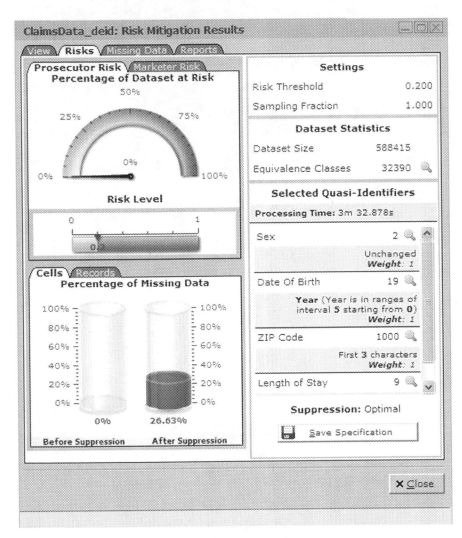

Figure 3: Save Specification for a De-identification

Finally, a masking specification can be created within the Masking Tool. Once you have specified all of the masking settings, you can use the "Save Specification" button to save the specification file (Figure 4). The specification can be used to mask any data set that contains the same fields.

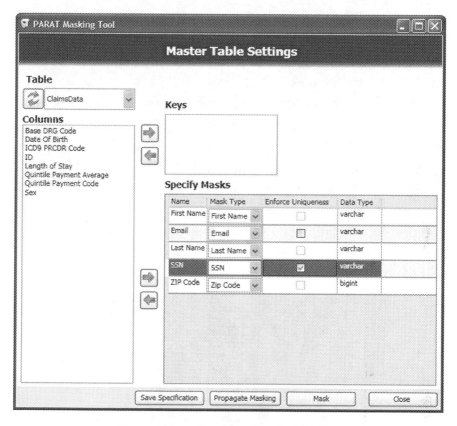

Figure 4: Save Specification for Masking

Executing Specifications from within PARAT

In this section I will show you how to execute a CSV import, a de-identification, and a database export specification sequentially from within PARAT. I am assuming you have already saved these specification files to your system.

To run a specification, select the "Execute Spec" item from the data menu. This will open the "Execute Specification" window.

First we add the import and risk mitigation specification (these can be added at the same time). Select the "CSV Import\Risk Mitigation" item from the specifications drop-down list and click the "Add" button. After adding the item, for the CSV Import you will need to specify the "Data File," the "Spec File," and the data set name to use to store the data within the database. Next you will need to specify the risk-mitigation spec file, as well as the data set name to use for the de-identified data set.

Finally we need to add the database export specification. From the specification drop-down list, select the "Database Export" item and click the "Add" button. You then need to select the database-export-specification file that you previously created.

Figure 5 shows all of these settings for a specification file that will import, de-identify, and export the "Claims Data" sample data set that is included with PARAT. After providing all the settings, click the process button to run the specification.

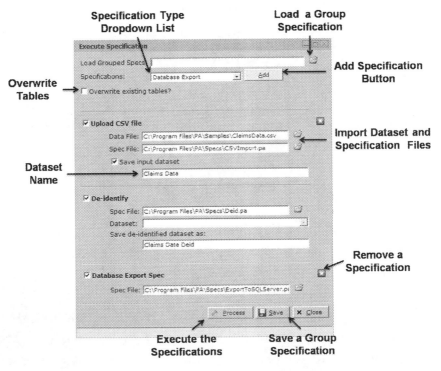

Figure 5: Import Specification Example

Group Specifications

A group-specification file allows you to store a series of specifications within a single file. This allows us to specify the entire de-identification process within a single group specification file. For example, we could group an import, a de-identification, and an export specification into a group specification file in order to automatically import a data set from a CSV file, process that data set, and then put the result in the appropriate location on the hard drive.

In our example from the previous section, after specifying all of the settings, we could create a group specification by clicking the "Save" button. Later on, to repeat the full process, we could reload the group specification file using the "Load Group Specification" button.

Executing Specifications from the Command Line

PARAT features a command line utility that allows us to run group specification files. This is particularly useful if you want to run group specifications on a regular interval since the commands can be executed regularly using a scheduler such as the windows scheduler.

To execute a group specification from the command line, run PARAT's command line tool while specifying a group specification file as an argument. For example, the following command will run a group specification that I saved to my hard drive.

```
"'C:\Program Files\PA\paratcmdln.exe'
'C:\Program Files\PA\Specs\GroupedSpec.pa'"
```

A command window will be displayed showing the progress of the execution and a log file will be created in the same folder as the grouped specification.

Of course, this can also be embedded within scripts that perform pre- and post-processing on the data sets. For example, some of our users embed command line calls within R scripts which perform more advanced analytics on the generated de-identified files—all within the same batch job.

PARAT allows the user to run multiple jobs concurrently (up to five in the default configuration). This makes it possible to have multiple command line batch jobs executing at the same time. This is particularly powerful for large data feeds or when performing a simulation. You just need to make sure that your hardware can handle the processing demands.

Editing Specifications

Specification can be manually edited using a text editor. This allows you to change the settings of a specification file. This can be done for individual specification files or group specification files.

This is particularly useful for group specification files, since they point at different data files and specification files on a hard drive. So, for example, if the path of a data file were to change you could edit the path directly within the group specification file instead of having to create a new file.

Conclusion

With PARAT's specification system for batch processing, continuous masking and de-identification is simple and intuitive. It allows for repeatable and predictable processes and results under a variety of user scenarios.

PARAT FUNCTIONALITY: PSEUDONYMS

Grant Middleton

Introduction

In two of our previous articles, "PARAT Functionality: Data Masking" and "PARAT Functionality: Maintaining Integrity When Masking a Multi-table Data Set," we introduced PARAT's masking functionality as a tool to help de-identify data. One of the features of PARAT's data-masking tool (DMT) is the ability to create pseudonyms.

Pseudonyms allow the owner of a data set to link records from multiple de-identified data sets. This is useful when new data for a specific patient or subset of patients is added to the database at a later point. The pseudonym can be used to find and link the patients' original record to the new data set. Pseudonyms can also be used, if required, to determine the identity of a de-identified record. This form of re-identification occurs when there is a need to notify a patient of a test result or when a patient wishes to withdraw their data from a database.

The DMT provides three methods for creating pseudonyms. The first involves masking a field using unique values for each patient, or the Unique Field Method. The second involves masking a field using the DMT's Pseudonym Masking Type. Finally, the third allows for the creation of Compound Pseudonyms on multiple fields. The method you choose will depend on the use case for the pseudonym and the data type of the field.

Unique Field Method: When All the Data Is Currently Available

If you are creating a pseudonym in a data set where all the data is currently available, you will use the Unique Field method. This approach is only useful when the creation of the pseudonym is a onetime event. If you need to repeat the process on any future data sets and require the pseudonyms to be consistent across data sets, you will want to use the method shown in the next section.

The unique field method involves creating unique random alphanumeric values to replace each value in the specific field chosen. For example, if the field chosen is a medical record number (MRN), for each MRN in the data set a new random alphanumeric value will be chosen. This method ensures that each instance of a value will have the same pseudonym. It will also guarantee that two different MRN values do not end up with the same pseudonym. Therefore, the integrity of the data will be maintained.

To create the pseudonym within the DMT, select the unique identifier field (e.g., MRN, SSN, etc.) and choose the "Enforce Uniqueness" option for that field (figure 1). Within the "Format" field, you need to provide the format for the mask. The number of unique values that can be generated from the format must be large enough to create a unique value for each record. For example, if you have fifty thousand records, the format must allow for at least fifty thousand unique values.

Specify Masks

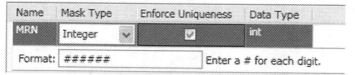

Name	Mask Type	Enforce Uniqueness	Data Type
MRN	Integer ▾	☑	int
	Format: ######		Enter a # for each digit.

Figure 1: Enforce Uniqueness Option

If you would like to apply the same pseudonym consistently to multiple tables, you will need to do masking propagation. (Please see "PARAT Functionality: Maintaining Integrity When Masking a Multi-table Data Set" regarding how to use the DMT's propagation features in Section VI.)

Pseudonym Masking Type: When the Pseudonym Needs to Be Repeatable

If you need to repeat the pseudonym over time, you will want to use the DMT's Pseudonym Masking Type. The pseudonym mask is a hash function which generates a hash on each value in the data set. The user provides a "salt" value, which acts like a password. Running the mask on the same value, using the same salt value, will always produce the same result. This allows the same pseudonym to be generated at any point in time.

This method allows you to match and/or find records within the de-identified data set when needed. This is possible because the pseudonym mask is repeatable. So you can take the value that you would like to find, turn it into a pseudonym, and then use that value to match the specific record in the data set.

To create a hash-based pseudonym within the DMT, select the unique identifier field (e.g., SSN) and the mask type of "Pseudonym" (figure 2). A salt value will be automatically provided, but you can change this as needed. If you would like to produce the same pseudonym in the future, you will need to use the same salt value, so save the salt value in a secure location.

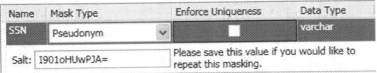

Figure 2: Pseudonym Masking Type

Again, if you would like to propagate the pseudonym to multiple tables in the database, you will need to do masking propagation. A description of how to do this can be found in the article "PARAT Functionality: Maintaining Integrity When Masking a Multi-table" in Section VI referenced previously.

The primary difference between the two types of pseudonyms, in addition to them meeting the requirements for two different use cases, are that the pseudonym based on the hash value: (a) tends to be longer and therefore consumes more space, and (b) requires you to keep the salt (or key) in a safe place.

Compound Pseudonyms: When Creating a Unique Identifier from Multiple Fields

A Compound Pseudonym allows a pseudonym to be generated from multiple fields in a data set. If there are multiple fields that combine to create a unique identifier, they can be turned into a single pseudonym using the compound pseudonym feature of PARAT.

Under the Database Masking menu, select the "Compound Pseudonym" button. The next step is to choose the data set for which you would like to generate the pseudonym.

In the compound pseudonym window (figure 3), you need to specify a new name for the compound pseudonym field by selecting the fields you would like to include in the compound pseudonym, and specify the salt value. A salt will be automatically provided for you, but you can change this as needed.

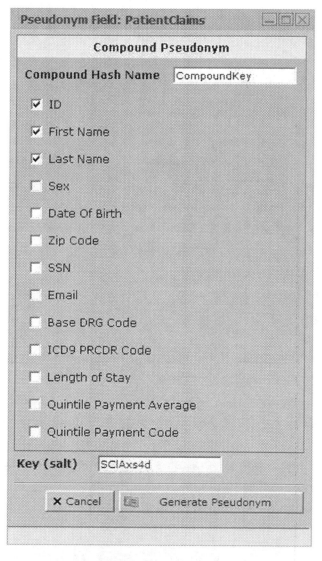

Figure 3: Compound Pseudonym Window

Linking Tables

A linking table includes the pseudonym and the original unique identifier values. This table can then be stored securely by the data owner and used to determine the identity of a record in the de-identified data set. A linking table is important when using the first method discussed in this article (using the Unique Field Method). A linking table is particularly useful, for example, if you need to link new data with the de-identified data, or if you needed to determine who a patient was in order to contact that patient.

Within PARAT, a linking table can be created in four simple steps:

1. Clone the identifier field(s) that will be used for the pseudonym. The cloned field allows us to manipulate the original field without completely erasing the identifier(s). PARAT features a clone field option within the Modify Fields tool. The Modify Fields tool is under the Database Management menu.
2. Generate the pseudonym on the cloned identifier field(s), leaving the original identifiers intact.
3. Export the pseudonym field and the original identifiers. This exported data is now the linking table. It contains the pseudonym and the original identifiers. If the data is exported to a CSV file, this file can also be encrypted by PARAT to secure the linking information.
4. Delete the original identifier(s) from the data set. The resulting data set contains the pseudonyms and no longer contains the identifiers. Once the rest of the data set has been de-identified, it can be sent to its intended recipient.

Conclusion

In this article, we have shown you how PARAT can be used to create pseudonyms of both integer and string fields, how to create compound pseudonyms from multiple fields, and how to create linking tables that can be used by the data custodian to link de-identified records with the original records. These features greatly aid both the de-identification process and the management of de-identified data. They give data custodians more control over their data while still maintaining the highest level of security and privacy standards.

RISK ASSESSMENT WIZARD—DETERMINING A RE-IDENTIFICATION RISK THRESHOLD

Grant Middleton

Introduction

One of the difficult decisions that needs to be made during data de-identification is how much de-identification to apply. If the data custodian de-identifies too much, the utility of the data decreases unnecessarily; too little and the data may be exposed to more risk than the data custodian had anticipated. The data also must meet the requirements in the HIPAA Privacy Rule Statistical Method for de-identification, which stipulates the risk must be "very small."

PARAT is able to measure the re-identification risk of a data set. When de-identifying a data set it is necessary to define a re-identification risk threshold that is acceptable to the data custodian. If the measured re-identification risk is above the threshold, the data needs to be de-identified to bring it below the threshold. The question then becomes how to define that threshold. Are there some norms that can be used as acceptable re-identification risk thresholds when disclosing health data? Are there good precedents that can be used?

The risk assessment wizard provides an objective framework in which to make this decision, matching the risk threshold to the context of the data. This methodology means the specifics of the data recipient(s) and the data itself must be taken into account when selecting the threshold. The wizard provides a repeatable and documented process to perform that analysis using validated checklists.

Methodology

The risk assessment wizard walks a user through a series of checklists and multiple-choice questions. Each question has an effect on the overall results of the assessment. The assessment is broken down into three different dimensions. The results of each dimension are combined, based on a risk matrix, and tell us the amount of risk exposure we can accept when releasing the data set (Figure 1).

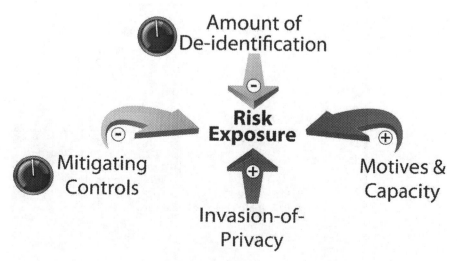

Figure 1: High-Level Risk Assessment Process

The mitigating controls dimension looks at the data recipients' safeguards, processes and procedures, and organizational transparency associated with their handling of personal data. Motives and Capacity looks at the motives and capacity of the data recipient to re-identify the data. Invasion of privacy looks at the characteristics of the actual data, including the sensitivity, the potential injury to patients, and the appropriateness of consent.

The wizard's questionnaire was built from the ground up, based on an analysis of privacy policies and REB guidelines across many small and large organizations. The results were then mapped to some of the major standards (ISO, Cobit, GAPP, HIPAA Security Rule, etc.).

The wizard can produce four possible risk threshold results that range from .05 (most amount of de-identification) to 0.33 (least amount of de-identification) (Figure 2). The amount of de-identification applied to a data set will change quite considerably when comparing the higher and lower risk thresholds, so it is important to get a defensible result.

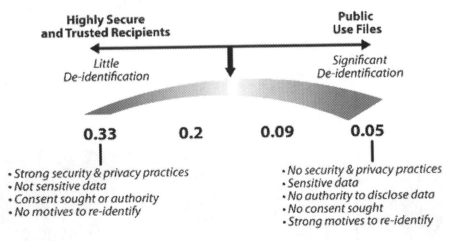

Figure 2: Risk Threshold Range

Using the Wizard

The first step is to determine whether the data will be released to the public. This determines which sections of the questionnaire will be shown (some sections are not applicable when releasing to the public). This choice will open up the main interface of the wizard shown in Figure 3.

1. Section Tabs: allow you to switch between the different sections
2. Subsection Buttons: allow you to choose the subsection
3. Menu Buttons: include New, Load, Save, Sensitivity Analysis, and Help
4. Questionnaire Map: a clickable map that can be used to navigate through the questionnaire. This tool also indicates question-completion status.
5. Overall Progress: indicates the total progress of the questionnaire
6. Question Buttons: allow you to show\hide comments and info
7. Navigation Buttons: allow you to move forward and backward through the questions

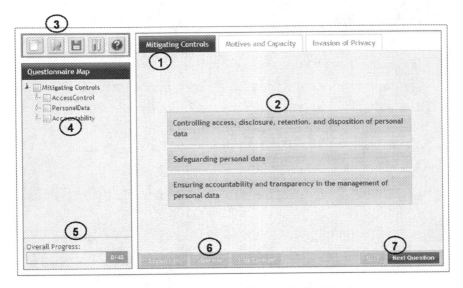

Figure 3: Risk Assessment Wizard Main Interface

After selecting a section and subsection, you will be presented with the first question in the section (Figure 4). Each question presents checkboxes and radio buttons that indicate potential responses to the overall question. When a question has been answered, the question text will be highlighted with a color indicating the question is complete. The color of the highlighted text will indicate the impact that question has on the risk, with red being high impact and green being low impact. You can click the "Next Question" button to move to the next question, or use the "Questionnaire Map" to switch to another question at any point. The questionnaire map on the side of the screen will give you an indication of what still needs to be completed.

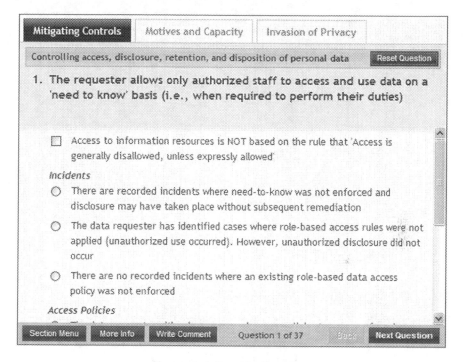

Figure 4: A Sample Question

For each question, you can write a comment or annotation (Figure 5) that will be associated with the question. This can be used to qualify the response given to the question. The annotation will be included with the question/response when the results are exported from the tool.

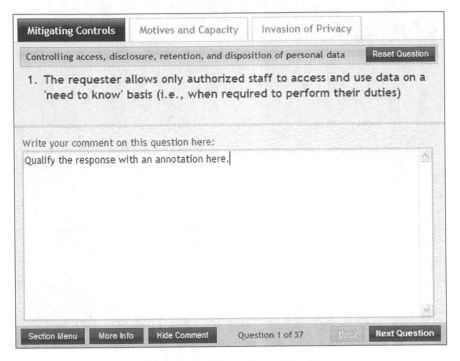

Figure 5: Annotate a Question with a Comment

Associated with each question is a "More Info" section (figure 6). This section provides a mapping of the question to different standards, such as ISO, Cobit, GAPP, HIPAA Security Rule, etc., including the relevant section of the standard. This can be very helpful in interpreting and understanding each question.

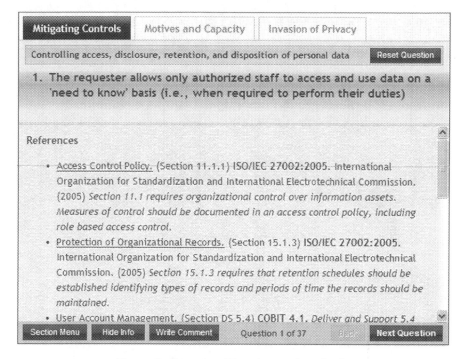

Figure 6: Question Mapping to Standards

Results

When the questionnaire is complete you can calculate the risk threshold. This will open the results view (Figure 7). This view will give you an indication of the risk impact for each section, as well as the recommended risk threshold value. You can view each of the questions and their responses on this page, as well as print and save the results.

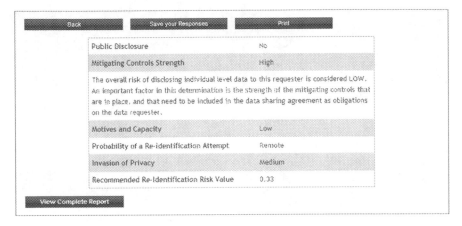

Figure 7: Risk Assessment Results

Sensitivity Analysis

A sensitivity analysis can be run once the questionnaire is complete. This analysis will give you an indication of how much the risk analysis would change based on changing any given question. For example, if you answered the questions with a pessimistic viewpoint, you can see how much of an affect this had on the results.

For each section, the sensitivity analysis report (Figure 8) will provide you with feedback that will guide the results toward the different risk boundaries. For example, it could indicate that to reach the low-risk boundary you would need to move one high risk answer to medium risk. The different tabs and buttons can be used to navigate each section of the report.

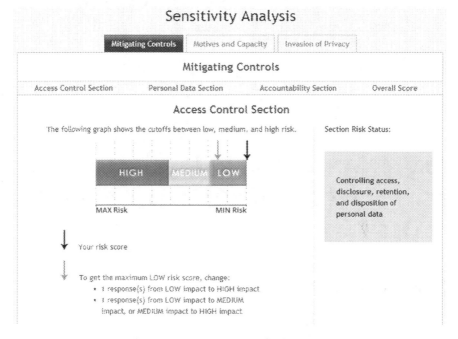

Figure 8: Sensitivity Analysis Report

Conclusion

The risk assessment wizard provides users with the ability to determine the risk threshold that should be applied when de-identifying and releasing data. Using a qualitative methodology, the questions guide you to a defensible quantitative risk threshold. The sensitivity analysis section helps you evaluate your responses and compare those to known risk boundaries. The goal of the tool is to help you determine a defensible risk threshold that meets your de-identification needs in a repeatable, objective, and documented manner.

DATE MANIPULATION AND CUSTOM HIERARCHIES WITH PARAT

Grant Middleton

Introduction

PARAT provides a number of tools that can be used to help prepare a data set for de-identification. Two of the newest additions to PARAT are the Date Transformation Tool and the Value Grouper Tool.

The Date Transformation Tool allows a user to run many different manipulation\extraction operations on date fields. The Value Grouping Tool allows a user to create custom groupings from the data within a field in a data set. These custom groupings can then be used as levels within a generalization hierarchy during de-identification.

Date Transformation Tool

The Date Transformation Tool (Figure 1) features four different date transformation types:

- **Date Extraction**—This allows the different parts of a date to be extracted from a date field (e.g., year, quarter, day, etc.)—for example, year value could be extracted from a birth date in order to create a new field with only the year of birth.

- **Date Arithmetic**—This allows addition or subtraction to be executed on a date field. The arithmetic can be performed at any granularity (e.g., year, day, month, etc.) using a fixed value or values from a different column.

- **Date Difference within a Column**—This allows the date differences to be calculated on a column using an anchored date or a running difference. For example, the difference between all dates and the first chronological date in the data set could be calculated.

- **Date Difference between Two Columns**—This allows the date differences between two columns to be calculated. The difference can be shown with at any granularity (e.g., difference as years, days, seconds, etc.).

Figure 1: Date Transformation Tool Interface

The tool provides a preview button that can be used to preview the results of any operation. This allows the outcome of the operation to be tested without running the tool on the full data set, saving precious time.

Date Transformation Example

In this example, we will calculate the difference in days between the date of diagnosis and the date of first treatment in a sample cancer treatment data set.

Figure 2 shows the settings used for calculating the difference between two columns. Here are the steps to follow to get the same settings:

- First we select the appropriate data set from the data set drop-down menu.
- We then select the "Date Difference between Columns" transformation option.
- We select the source column, which is the date of first treatment field.
- We select the subtractor column, which is the date of diagnosis field.
- We select the difference as type, which is day.
- Finally, we specify the new column name, "DateDifferenceDiagnosisTreatment_Day."

DateOfFirstTreatment	DateOfDiagnosis	DateDifferenceDiagnosisTreatment_Day
12/22/2011 12:00:00 AM	11/20/2011 12:00:00 AM	32
11/21/2011 12:00:00 AM	11/7/2011 12:00:00 AM	14
11/14/2011 12:00:00 AM	10/20/2011 12:00:00 AM	25
11/10/2011 12:00:00 AM	10/28/2011 12:00:00 AM	13
7/19/2011 12:00:00 AM	5/30/2011 12:00:00 AM	50
8/9/2011 12:00:00 AM	6/10/2011 12:00:00 AM	60
12/17/2011 12:00:00 AM	11/24/2011 12:00:00 AM	23
4/2/2011 12:00:00 AM	3/21/2011 12:00:00 AM	12
2/23/2011 12:00:00 AM	1/2/2011 12:00:00 AM	52
4/18/2011 12:00:00 AM	2/22/2011 12:00:00 AM	55
5/12/2011 12:00:00 AM	4/28/2011 12:00:00 AM	14
12/8/2011 12:00:00 AM	10/17/2011 12:00:00 AM	52
1/6/2012 12:00:00 AM	11/20/2011 12:00:00 AM	47
8/5/2011 12:00:00 AM	7/6/2011 12:00:00 AM	30
8/22/2011 12:00:00 AM	7/26/2011 12:00:00 AM	27
6/17/2011 12:00:00 AM	4/25/2011 12:00:00 AM	53
10/7/2011 12:00:00 AM	8/18/2011 12:00:00 AM	50
8/22/2011 12:00:00 AM	8/12/2011 12:00:00 AM	10
11/19/2011 12:00:00 AM	9/21/2011 12:00:00 AM	59
6/11/2011 12:00:00 AM	5/25/2011 12:00:00 AM	17

Figure 2: Date Difference between Column Settings

By running a preview of this manipulation, we can see what the outcome will look like in Figure 3. If the preview is unacceptable and results in values of negative date difference, then we need to switch the source column and subtractor fields in the settings. If the preview is acceptable, we can then run the transformation. The result will be a new column in the data set that contains the number of days between the date of diagnosis and the date of treatment.

Figure 3: Date Difference Preview

Value Grouper Tool

PARAT's Value Grouping Tool (Figure 4) allows users to create custom groupings. This is useful for fields where a standard hierarchy (e.g., date\integer ranges, cropping characters, etc.) is not satisfactory. This could be the case when no simple hierarchy exists (e.g., race, ethnicity, etc.) or when we want to specifically assign values to different groups (e.g., grouping ages into categories such as child, teenager, or adult, or into nonstandard ranges such as 0-10, 11-20, 21-65, etc.). The groupings produced by the tool can be used within PARAT as levels in a hierarchy when de-identifying a data set.

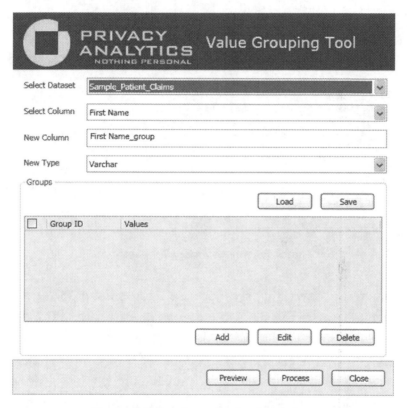

Figure 4: Value Grouping Tool Interface

Creating a Custom Grouping

In this example, we are going to create a custom grouping for a set of languages.

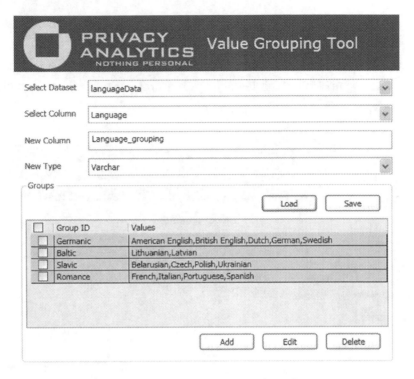

Figure 5: Value Grouping Tool Settings

Figure 5 shows the settings used for creating the custom hierarchy. Here are the steps to follow to get the same settings:

1. We first select the source data set that contains the data that we will use to create the hierarchy. This is done by using the "Select Data Set" drop-down menu. We have selected the "Language Data" data set.
2. We now select the specific column using the "Select Column" drop-down menu. We have selected the "Language" column.
3. Enter a name for the new column that will contain the hierarchy in the "New Column" text box. We are using the column "Language_grouping."

4. Select the type that will be used for the new field. In this case, we have chosen Varchar.

5. For each grouping that we want to create, we need to follow steps 6 through 9.

6. We then click the "Add" button to add new groupings to the hierarchy. This opens the "Group Creator" window (Figure 6).

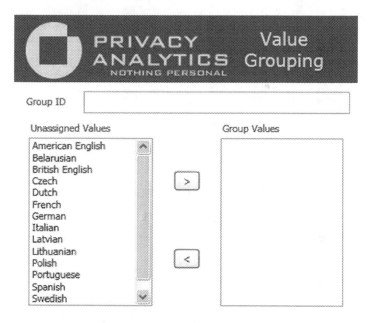

Figure 6: Group Creator Window

7. We enter the group value into the "Group ID" text field. For example, we have created the group "Germanic."

8. For each value in the "Unassigned Values" list that is part of the grouping, we move it to the "Group Values" section. We have selected the values American English, British English, Dutch, German, and Swedish for the group "Germanic" (Figure 7).

9. We then click OK to add the new grouping.

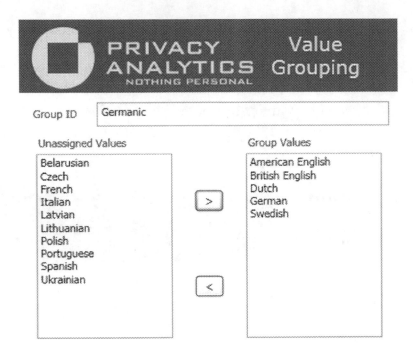

Figure 7: Germanic Grouping

After we have set up the groupings, we can click on the "Preview" button to generate a preview (Figure 8). This allows us to verify the outcome on a small set of the data before running the grouping on the full data set. If the preview is acceptable, we click the "Process" button to create the custom grouping.

PRIVACY ANALYTICS
NOTHING PERSONAL
Preview

Language	Language_grouping	
American English	Germanic	
French	Romance	
Dutch	Germanic	
Spanish	Romance	
British English	Germanic	
German	Germanic	
Spanish	Romance	
Dutch	Germanic	
British English	Germanic	
Dutch	Germanic	
Polish	Slavic	
Spanish	Romance	
French	Romance	
British English	Germanic	
British English	Germanic	
Czech	Slavic	
Swedish	Germanic	
French	Romance	
Spanish	Romance	
Spanish	Romance	

Figure 8: Value Grouping Preview

Using a Custom Grouping during De-identification

A custom grouping field created with the Value Grouping Tool can be used as a hierarchy when de-identifying a data set in PARAT. To add the custom grouping field to the hierarchy, click the "Add a field as a hierarchy" button as seen in Figure 9. Then choose the specific field that will be used for the hierarchy. Only fields that are not selected as a quasi-identifier can be used as a level in the hierarchy.

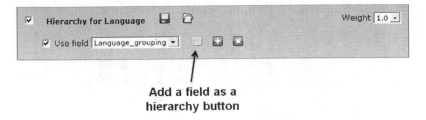

**Add a field as a
hierarchy button**

Figure 9: Using a Field as a Level in a Hierarchy

Conclusion

The creation of the Date Transformation and Value Grouping tools add even more flexibility to PARAT's suite of data management tools. They provide the ability to easily mold your data into a form suited to your specific needs—all this while ensuring the risk related to the data falls below the threshold you set.

SECTION VII

Author Biographies

Luk Arbuckle

Luk Arbuckle is a statistician with the Electronic Health Information Laboratory (EHIL) at the CHEO Research Institute and is a consultant to Privacy Analytics. He holds a master's of science in statistics from the University of Ottawa, and a master's of science in mathematics from the University of Guelph. Among his many academic honors and awards are a Canada graduate scholarship, and a postgraduate scholarship from the Natural Sciences and Engineering Research Council of Canada.

D Barth-Jones

Daniel C. Barth-Jones is a Statistical Disclosure Control researcher and HIV Epidemiologist. He serves as an Assistant Professor of Clinical Epidemiology at the Mailman School of Public Health at Columbia University in New York and an Adjunct Assistant Professor and Epidemiologist at the Wayne State University School of Medicine in Detroit, Michigan. Dr. Barth-Jones received his Ph.D. degree in Epidemiology from the University of Michigan. Dr. Barth-Jones' work on statistical disclosure science has focused the importance of properly balancing two vital public policy goals: effectively protecting individuals's privacy and preserving the scientific accuracy of statistical and geo-statistical analyses conducted with de-identified health data. His public health research focuses on the areas of HIV and infectious disease epidemic modeling and simulation, and health economic evaluations of public health policies for vaccination and other preventative intervention programs.

K El Emam

Dr. Khaled El Emam is the founder and CEO of Privacy Analytics, Inc. He is also an associate professor at the University of Ottawa, Faculty of Medicine, a senior investigator at the Children's Hospital of Eastern Ontario Research Institute, and a Canada research chair in Electronic Health Information at the University of Ottawa. His main area of research is developing techniques for health data de-identification or anonymization and secure disease surveillance for public health purposes. He has made many contributions to the health privacy area. In addition, he has considerable experience de-identifying personal health information under the HIPAA Privacy Rule Statistical Standard.

Khaled was previously a senior research officer at the National Research Council of Canada, and prior to that he was head of the Quantitative Methods Group at the Fraunhofer Institute in Kaiserslautern, Germany. He has cofounded two companies to commercialize the results of his research work. In 2003 and 2004, he was ranked as the top systems and software engineering scholar worldwide by the Journal of Systems and Software based on his research on measurement and quality evaluation and improvement, and ranked second in 2002 and 2005. He holds a PhD from the Department of Electrical and Electronics Engineering, King's College, at the University of London (UK). His website is www.ehealthinformation.ca.

A Fineberg

Anita Fineberg, LLB, CIPP/C, is a sole practitioner and consultant specializing in the areas of privacy, access to information, data security, and information management issues. She focuses on health information privacy and the use of health information in the development of electronic medical and health records and has a particular interest in the use of health information for research and de-identification of data. Anita advises private and public-sector clients on compliance with PIPEDA, PHIPA, other Canadian provincial privacy legislation, health information privacy requirements, and global data protection laws, as well as on the management of the access to information process under FIPPA and comparable legislation in other provinces.

J Giszczak

James J. Giszczak, a member with McDonald Hopkins, litigates matters involving data security and data privacy and advises clients regarding data security measures and responding to security breaches. Jim also works with clients in a myriad of industries to assess and implement appropriate data security safeguards and continues to work with federal, state, and local authorities, as well as third-party vendors. Jim can be reached at jgiszczak@mcdonaldhopkins.com.

Rebecca Herold is The Privacy Professor (www.privacyguidance.com) & Virtual CPO/CISO for Compliance Helper clients (www.compliancehelper.com).

R Herold

Jay Innes

Jay Innes is a reporter and documentary maker by training. He was responsible for marketing at Privacy Analytics, Inc.

Elizabeth Jonker

Elizabeth Jonker is the research coordinator and privacy officer for the Electronic Health Information Laboratory at the CHEO Research Institute. She was recently certified as a CIPP/C with the International Association of Privacy Professionals. Elizabeth graduated magna cum laude from the University of Ottawa with an honors BA in philosophy with a second concentration in psychology. Prior to her role with the Electronic Health Information Laboratory, she coordinated children's programs with the city of Ottawa.

Dennis Melamed is president of Melamedia, LLC, a regulatory affairs research and publishing company. He is the editor and publisher of *Health Information Privacy/Security Alert*, a monthly industry newsletter that has focused on health data stewardship issues since 1997. He is also an adjunct professor at the Drexel College of Medicine, where he teaches courses on biomedical product regulation.

D Melamed

Grant Middleton

Grant Middleton is a product deployment specialist at Privacy Analytics Inc. He received his master of science in electronic business technologies from the University of Ottawa in 2009. He received a bachelor of computing with a subject of specialization in software design from Queen's University in 2007.

Kirk J. Nahra is a partner with Washington, DC-based Wiley Rein LLP where he specializes in privacy, information security, and insurance litigation and counseling. He is chair of the firm's privacy practice and cochairs its health-care practice. He has served on the board for the International Association for Privacy Professionals and is the editor of the IAPP's *The Privacy Advisor* monthly newsletter. He is a graduate of Georgetown University and the Harvard Law School and is a frequent author and speaker on privacy and security issues.

K Nahra

An associate with McDonald Hopkins in Detroit, Michigan, Dominic A. Paluzzi advises clients regarding data privacy and network security measures. He also drafts information security programs, incident response plans, and responds to data security breaches. Dominic coaches clients who have experienced a data breach, ensuring compliance and minimizing exposure. Dominic can be reached at dpaluzzi@mcdonaldhopkins.com.

D Paluzzi

K Pastoor

Kevin J. Pastoor, CPCU is a managing director with Aon Corporation, the leading global provider of risk management, insurance, and reinsurance brokerage, as well as human resource consulting and outsourcing. Kevin provides risk and insurance placement advice to clients in a variety of industries including manufacturing, construction, higher education, and health care. Kevin can be reached at Kevin. Pastoor@aon.com.

G Peterson

Grant Peterson is a HIPAA privacy and security consultant with more than twelve years' experience as a chief compliance officer and consultant. Grant specializes in the HITECH Act and HIPAA privacy and security audits, and the implementation and attestation to health-care organizations and business associates. Grant holds a BS in public administration from Minnesota State University, and a Juris Doctor from Hamline University School of Law.

K Rashbaum

Kennneth N. Rashbaum, Esq., is an attorney in New York City. His practice focuses on counsel to health-care providers and life-sciences corporations on privacy and security compliance and implementation. He has more than twenty-five years' experience in health care and the pharmaceutical industry as a litigator, trial lawyer, and counselor, has presented numerous Grand Rounds and in-service lectures on a spectrum of compliance issues, and speaks and writes across the United States on health information system, privacy and security, and operational design. Visit www.rashbaumassociates.com.

A Waldo

Ms. Waldo's law practice is focused on privacy, information security, and health-care issues. She is experienced in advising clients regarding privacy compliance, risk management, information security, marketing, international data transfers, and integrating privacy goals into business strategies. She counsels and represents clients regarding public policy, external relations, and government relations matters in the fields of privacy and health care.

Ms. Waldo served as an in-house lawyer for much of her career. She was the global chief privacy officer for Lenovo, a large international computer manufacturer, where she was responsible for compliance with privacy laws applicable to marketing, human resources, international data transfers, and product development. She also represented the company's public policy positions in domestic and international privacy conferences and negotiations. She previously led privacy compliance as chief privacy officer for Hoffmann-La Roche, a large international pharmaceutical company, and worked in public policy for GlaxoSmithKline, providing legislative support on privacy and other matters. She was actively involved with the International Pharmaceutical Privacy Consortium. She served as in-house counsel at IBM, working on consumer protection, marketing, and e-business. Prior to her work at IBM, she had been a commercial litigator and had handled tax legislation for a state legislature.

She counsels clients on consumer-law privacy matters, which apply to businesses in general, as well as privacy laws specific to the health-care sector (HIPAA and HITECH). She has particular interest in and experience with emerging technologies that handle sensitive health information, such as personal health records, genetics-related companies, and Health Information Exchanges. She has served on the Personal Health Record work group for the Certification Commission on Health Information Technology, has advised a state Health Information Exchange, and currently serves on the board of advisors for the Harvard SHARP grant on substitutable electronic health record components.

A frequent public speaker, Ms. Waldo is active in the International Association of Privacy Professionals and the Carolina Privacy Officials Network, has consulted with foreign governments regarding privacy laws, and has represented the US government in APEC privacy talks in Korea and Australia. She is a Certified Information Privacy Professional.

SECTION VIII

Acronyms

AES—Advanced Encryption Standard

AG—Attorney General

APEC—Asia-Pacific Economic Corporation

CAN-SPAM—Controlling the Assault of Non-Solicited Pornography and Marketing Act of 2003

CDT—Center for Democracy and Technology

CFR—Code of Federal Regulations

CHEO—Children's Hospital of Eastern Ontario

CIHR—Canadian Institutes of Health Research

CIPP/C—Certified Information Privacy Professional/Canada

CISO—Chief Information Security Officer

CMS—Centers for Medicare and Medicaid Services

COACH—Canada's Health Information Association

COBIT—IT Governance Framework

COPPA—Children's Online Privacy Protection Act

DAD—Discharge Access Database

DMT—Data Masking Tool

EHIL—Electronic Health Information Laboratory

EMR—Electronic Medical Record

EPHIPA—E-Health Personal Health Information Access and Protection of Privacy Act

FD&C Act—Federal Food, Drug and Cosmetic Act

FIPPA—Freedom of Information and Protection of Privacy Act

FIPS—Federal Information Processing Standard

FOIPA—Freedom of Information and Protection of Privacy Act

FTC—Federal Trade Commission

GAPP—Generally Accepted Privacy Principles

GIC—Massachusetts Group Insurance Commission

GLBA—Gramm-Leach-Bliley Act

HHS—Department of Health and Human Services

HIPAA—Health Insurance Portability and Accountability Act

HIT—Health Information Technology

HITECH—Health Information Technology for Economic and Clinical Health Act

IAPP—International Association of Privacy Professionals

IPC—Information and Privacy Commissioner of Ontario

IRB—Institutional Review Board

ITERA—Identity Theft Enforcement and Restitution Act

NIST—National Institute of Standards and Technology
OCR—Office for Civil Rights
PARAT—Privacy Analytics Risk Assessment Tool
PCI—Payment Card Industry
PCI DSS—Payment Card Industry Data Security Standards
PHI—Personal Health Information
PHIPA—Personal Health Information Protection Act
PHR—Personal Health Record
PI—Personal Information
PII—Personally Identifying Information
PIPEDA—Personal Information Protection and Electronic Documents Act
PUMF—Public Use Microdata File
REB—Research Ethics Board

INDEX